Living, Laughing and Loving Life!

Living, Laughing and Loving Life!

Dan Miller

with Jeanne Zornes

WinePress Publishing
MUKILTEO, WA 98275

About the Cover

One winter day, our son Sky caught a steelhead in the Wenatchee River and asked me to take this picture.

When I showed the fishy "priorities" picture in my humorous speaking presentations, we received many requests for copies. We decided to make it into an 11 X 14 poster, with all the proceeds

Priorities

going to (the baby) Audrey's college fund. By the time she was ten years old, she had $30,000 for her education from that picture!

By the way, Audrey *loves* to go fishing with her dad. Right side up, of course!

Want a copy? Call Audrey's grandma (Judy) at 1-360-871-8446 ($8.00).

Audrey and one of her many fish

To Judy —

my biggest dreammaker,

my best friend, and my love.

You are the wind beneath my wings.

Contents

Acknowledgments

This book has stories about several of my dreams—dreams which came true because of "Dreammakers" who believed in me and gave me the encouragement to take risks, persist, laugh and live my dreams. I give God credit as my Master Dreammaker, but there are others whom I want to mention.

♥ Herb and Bodell Miller, my mom and dad, who started me in believing that I was special.

♥ Judy, who has made my life very special and a great adventure. She is my #1 dreammaker and the wind beneath my wings.

♥ Judy's mom, "Gram," who became my mom. She has been a great support and a true blessing.

♥ Sky, Danica and Karmen, our children, who have given us much joy and continue to be our best friends.

♥ Carmen Bossenbrock, physical therapist, our Karmen's namesake, who put me back on my feet.

♥ Jeanne Zornes, who with her special writing gifts, insight, and great sense of humor, helped make this book a reality.

♥ Lois Lyon, Linden Schuyler, G. David Knutson, Sky, and Suze Marie Kroeker, who spent their valuable time editing for me.

—Dan

Introduction

Ten years ago, I was asked to share some of my experiences in overcoming my bout with polio at age eighteen. I was pleased with the positive response I received. Soon I was asked to share with other groups. The response was the same, a standing ovation. When I asked myself why, I realized that many people have lost hope. They are weary, discouraged, stressed out, and beaten down by life's negatives. Fun and laughter have slipped out of their lives. Some have lost sight of their dreams. Many people need to be reminded to choose to enjoy life, and to laugh more, in spite of their problems. My stories help them to make those choices.

In 1990 I began speaking full time, sharing my stories of hope and encouragement. In my first six years I gave 800 presentations to more than 250,000 people. Many asked for a book, giving me a new dream to pursue. That dream is now in your hands.

I hope this book will help you renew your dreams, and give you the courage to risk, live, laugh, love, and persist in life.

—Dan

Foreword

Greetings! I love it when famous people ask me to write forewords for their autobiographies. However, I have never before written a foreword for a person as inspirational, witty, risky, funny and talented as Dan Miller. And I have never before written a foreword where I might eventually inherit a portion of the fortune generated by sales of the book. And, actually, I have never before written a foreword.

This book first describes the impact of the devastating and crippling illness of polio, on an exceptional young athlete in the prime of his life. The rest of the book summarizes how caring, supportive people—*Dreammakers*—

Sky's family: Pam, Skylin, Sky, Audrey, Heather & Haylie

gave this crippled athlete the confidence to achieve his goals beyond anyone's imagination.

You will read how his fun-filled attitude and Dreammaker wife helped build a successful career in teaching and school administration. And you will read about how a man with only one good arm and two bad legs could learn to fly a plane, golf, swim, shoot hoops and ride a motorcycle. You'll find that behind each fun story is a lesson in inner strength.

Dan Miller now travels full time as a motivational speaker—still teaching–how to live, laugh, and love life!

And don't feel sorry for Dan. I never have. Perhaps because I have been shown that life isn't strong arms and legs, but an inner choice and external support from *Dreammakers*. And don't pray for Dan to be healed. It would ruin his speaking career!

I know you'll like Dad's book. My hope is that you like it as much as I do.

—*Sky Miller*

Middleword

Growing up in the Miller household had its advantages and disadvantages. Advantages included growing up in an environment that encouraged laughter, positive thinking and talking, looking for the good or positive in every situation and knowing we were loved unconditionally.

The disadvantages? It was hard to feel sorry for yourself or get much sympathy. When I tried to feel sorry for myself, I remembered what Dad had gone through, and realized I took too many things for granted. It's hard to be depressed looking at life that way.

I still remember the time I realized how unusual our family was. Most dads change flat bike tires, build dog houses and move heavy items. My mom was the one who did all those things. She is truly the "great woman behind the man." Mom supported Dad through all his ideas,

Danica and Jay Kelly

risky ventures (flying an ultralight aircraft), physical struggles, and the highs and lows all families experience. She prefers not to be in the limelight, but silently sits by and admires all that Dad has done and become.

Mom and Dad are two of my best friends. They rejoice in my successes and cry with me in times of struggle. Through thick or thin, they always remain proud of me.

One huge lesson that my parents taught me is how to love. After 38 years of marriage, they are the exception to the rule in today's world. They still love each other and are role models to their children and grandchildren. Our families gather often for weekends of laughing, playing, and enjoying time with each other, practicing *Living, Laughing, and Loving Life.*

Being a Miller has not been easy, but I wouldn't trade my upbringing or family for anything. Through them I have learned to love, be a good wife, parent and friend. I thank God for you and all the lives you touch in a positive way. I love you!

—*Danica (Miller) Kelly*

Amanda and Andrew Kelly

Backword

I'm not really. Backwards that is. I believe this part should be called *the Finalword*. Since my parents always loved me best, I should have the final word, don't you think? I think this book is a terrific idea. Maybe with this book, more people can discover what *Living, Laughing, and Loving Life* is all about.

I thought everyone had laughter in their houses, and extra people hanging around. Later I realized it just wasn't so, and those people hanging around were drawn to Dad and Mom because they were fun. They were— *Dreammakers*.

I really did believe they loved me best, but as the years went by and bits of wisdom and maturity fought to get in, I realized that Danica and Sky always thought Mom and Dad loved THEM best. Isn't that a wonderful gift to give your children? Silent, unbreakable dreammaking in action. Make someone feel like the most important person ever created. Teach by example. Laugh a lot. Share your laughter with everyone.

The more I learn about life and living, the luckier I feel. I grew up surrounded by support and my own cheering section no matter what. Sometimes, being a dreammaker is keeping your mouth shut. Sometimes it is building confidence by pulling your kids out of class and having them demonstrate something for your P.E. class. Sometimes it is sacrificing by having one parent stay home with the kids when they are young. Sometimes it is laughing at yourself when you fall down.

Sometimes being a dreammaker happens by accident, though mostly it doesn't.

These are the types of things that Mom and Dad did for me and are now encouraging others to do for the special people around them. They are reaching further out with this book. What a great idea—to write Dad's story.

Karmen's family: Karmen, Kasey, Mitchell & Brent Harris

When I am fortunate enough to hear Dad speak, I am amazed at the reaction from the group. After all, it's just Dad. I am also touched, after all it's MY dad. I am also proud to be a part of such a terrific family. The message is real. And to think I thought every family was fun-loving and caring like mine!

Dad and Mom are top-notch *Dreammakers*. They still have time to follow their own dreams. As their child (their favorite, remember?) I am delighted to watch, and of course, have the Finalword.

This book was my idea!

—*Karmen (Miller) Harris*

1

—∿∿∼—

"Let's See What You Can Do!"

College adviser...Dreammaker or Dream-breaker?

I looked across the campus that freezing December day, never imagining my college years starting this way. I dug my Canadian (forearm) crutch into the snow–covered pathway and began one of the longest emotional walks of my life.

Eighteen months earlier I graduated from Pateros High School, in central Washington, firmly focused on my dream of becoming a physical education teacher. I loved sports and played every chance I could. I was a good athlete.

I was captain and an all–star player on a league championship basketball team that lost only two games. I played halfback and linebacker on football teams that went undefeated for three consecutive

years. I played second base on a championship baseball team. I also ran the mile as part of a track team that
took second place in the

Team captain, Dan;
Championship game 1955

district. (My coach used
to laugh and say, "Miller,
you're little but
you're...slow!")

Life was good in
high school. I graduated
in the top ten of my
class. (We had five girls
and five boys in our
senior class!) I was
accepted to attend
Eastern Washington
College of Education at
Cheney, near Spokane.
Just the summer stood
between me and the
beginning of what I

hoped to be the best years of my life.

I did not make it to college that year. Five weeks
after high school graduation, I contracted polio. For the
next 15 months, I was enrolled in two unexpected
classes of life. I called them Physical Therapy 101 and
Rehab 102. The legs that sprang for rebounds were now
80 percent paralyzed. The right arm that propelled jump
shots was virtually useless. My left arm, which now
gripped an elbow-high Canadian crutch, had about half
of its original muscle.

I no longer had an athlete's body as I began that slippery trip to the college fieldhouse that cold December
day. My registration packet was labeled "P.E. Exempt."

Dan and his '51 Ford. 1956

(I could have sold dozens of those hummers!) I was so unsteady that I fell a half dozen times trying to find the physical education professor assigned as my adviser.

I'm not sure what Dr. Richard Hagelin first thought as I wobbled into his office and plopped into a chair.

"I can't run or jump," I told him as I dropped my crutch. "I can't do push-ups or pull-ups. I can't climb a rope or jump rope, but I want to major in physical education and become a P.E. teacher."

I now wonder if he realized how much the rest of my life would hinge on his response. I knew he could say, "I'm sorry, Danny, you're in the wrong department." I couldn't lift either arm above my head. I couldn't throw a football or shoot a basket. I had no athletic skills and he knew it. But he didn't hesitate a moment.

He just smiled and said, *"Well, let's see what you can do."*

Wenatchee Valley Clinic

135 NORTH MISSION STREET
PHONE NORMANDY 3-5141
WENATCHEE, WASHINGTON

September 15, 1956

To Whom It May Concern:

Mr. Dan Miller was stricken with poliomyelitis in July, 1955 and as a result has severe weakness of his lower extremities and paralysis of his right upper extremity.

It would not be advisable for him to try to participate in any athletics and is unfit for military service.

Edward F. Cadman, M.D.

Doctor's advice: No athletics for Dan.

2

If God Didn't Want Us to Fly, He Would Have Given Us Roots

Early dreams

My life began January 29, 1937, in an apartment above a grocery-meat market in Bridgeport, Washington. I was delivered by "Nursey" Heatherington, a lady who did midwife honors for a lot of home births in our little farm town. She called me "Danny Boy" as soon as I was born, since my folks had already decided on Daniel after my great-grandfather Daniel Washburn, a horse-riding circuit preacher. My middle name, "Charles," honored my uncle, whose store-top apartment my parents were renting.

I did not always tell the truth about my middle name when I grew up. I remembered my Grandpa Miller's middle initial was "C" and he always told me it stood for "chicken." I continue to tease people with the same yarn.

I grew up in North Central Washington, in small towns named Bridgeport, Mansfield, and Pateros. I was a farm boy whose body was shaped by hard work and whose attitude was nurtured by down-to-earth parents who stood for solid values. They took me and my two younger sisters to church every Sunday. The farm was a wonderful place for a kid. We knew our responsibilities, but we could also run and hope and dream. One farm was about six miles from

Mansfield, a town of 300 people. I tell folks that we were so far out in the country, we had to go towards town to hunt!

When I was in fifth grade I began dreaming of someday flying my own plane. I bought and assembled model airplanes. I watched spray planes swoop over our farm crops. I always found an excuse to hang around the old dirt landing strip nearby,

Fifth grader, Dan, dreams about flying, and basketball stardom.

just soaking up the sounds and smells of those vintage planes.

I skipped classes once in high school when another classmate and I volunteered to "flag" for our local crop duster. We were positioned about a quarter mile apart. The big bi-wing Stearman plane lined up on us and dived down to ten feet above the wheat field, coming right at us. As the plane got within 200 to 300 feet, we began pacing the correct number of steps to position ourselves for its next pass, and to get out of the way as the plane zoomed past at more than 100 miles an hour. Then it would turn around and make another spray run right at us again. It was a wonderful, thrilling job—worth every nickel of the five dollars we earned that day.

The next day we were called into the principal's office for a good chewing-out and a swat with the paddle. I never skipped school again. I was hooked on airplanes, though, and grabbed other "flagging" jobs that didn't conflict with school hours.

I continued to dream of the day I would fly my own airplane. For high school graduation, my spray plane pilot friend "Spider" Anderson took me up in his Supercub and did rolls, loops, and spins right over my home. Spider was a daredevil pilot. He would entertain us at the Pateros Apple Pie Jamboree by shutting off his engine in mid-air. He then crawled outside on the strut, leaned forward, and hand-propped the plane's engine back to life. And, he

Dan's first airplane

was the only one in the plane! I was impressed. He said he would teach me to fly that summer. I marked the calendar with the date of my first lesson.

3

Dream-breaker–Polio

From star athlete to flat on my back

Grabbing a shower and dinner and then hopping into my '51 Ford for a Saturday night in town was all I could think of that hot July 9, 1955. There was a good movie and I was ready to hang out with my friends after a long, hard day raking hay on our farm.

Life was simply good. I was anticipating college and had the best part of my life ahead—years when I could pursue my many dreams: perfect my guitar-playing, maybe start a band, find that special girl to marry, raise talented and gifted kids, learn to fly an airplane...and, of course, become a P.E. teacher .

One fear families had in those days was a disease called polio or infantile paralysis. By that summer 60,000 kids had died of polio and another 600,000 were crippled. Dr. Jonas Salk had produced a vaccine that people were heralding as the end of the dreaded disease, and the vaccine was filtering through cities and towns. By April of

1955, forty-four states had distributed it. Eventually, it would reach Pateros, Washington, population 700.

As that summer afternoon wore down, I wore down with it. I felt increasingly sick, like I had the flu. I had taken off my shirt earlier that day to deepen my already

great suntan, but now my dusty body was streaked with sweat from both the heat and a rising fever. My neck hurt and felt stiff. I unhooked the old hay rake, pulled the tractor under a lean-to, turned it off, and struggled over to my Ford for the five-mile drive back home.

It was all I could do to drive. I told my mother I didn't feel like din-

High School Graduation 1955

ner, and headed down to my bedroom in the basement. She started to worry, for polio was still a word people whispered with dread. It struck without warning. As the night came on, I became increasingly sick, vomiting every few minutes into a bucket by my bed. My back and neck were in constant pain and my fever rose higher and higher.

Our family doctor lived close by, and hurried over to check on me. He hit my elbow and knee joints with his little hammer and found no reflexes.

" I think it's polio," he told my anxious parents. "We could take him in for a spinal tap and confirm it, but I'm pretty sure. Dan needs to be isolated. He is extremely contagious until the fever breaks."

The nearest hospital set up to handle polio was 60 miles away in Wenatchee. The other option was to isolate me at home until the fever broke. My parents decided to keep me at home.

I remember many hours of fever, vomiting and incredible pain racking my back and spinal column. Then one day I awoke unable to move my right arm— the same arm which had received such a healthy workout raking hay that Saturday. My left arm was next. The pain told me that my legs would soon be immovable. By the end of the week, all four limbs were useless. All I could move were my left wrist and fingers.

My world shrank to my small basement bedroom. One light bulb lit my dungeon of pain, and in the daytime, some light came through a one-by-two-foot window at the top of the basement's cement block wall.

My fever hung on for nearly two weeks. I was unable to even turn over in my bed. I had much difficulty urinating and no bowel movements—nothing would move!

I had to rely on Mom to feed me, wash me, and turn me over. I was like an 18-year-old baby.

Looking back, I am amazed Mom or my 16-year-old sister, Marlene, didn't contract polio from me. Marlene stayed at home and took over Mom's jobs of cooking, house and yard work, while Mom became my full-time nurse. Marlene also took over some of my farm work duties. My aunt Minnie Lee and uncle Kermit Stennes housed my younger sister Bonnie. Nobody else dared get near me. When people came to visit, they always kept that murky basement window between us. They would hunch down, cup their hands around their eyes, and stare down at me. I felt like I was on display at the zoo. In days, I had gone from being an athletic, confident teenager, ready for life, to a helpless "exhibit" of the ravages of polio. I also became a statistic—I was one of the last acute polio cases in Washington State. The Salk vaccine reached Pateros soon after I became sick.

It seemed as though I lost my whole body. To keep from getting discouraged, I thought of how much I had: supportive parents and sisters and wonderful people praying for me. I was also praying that somehow I would be spared a few muscles. That didn't seem possible, though, after my two weeks in solitary confinement. My body was as stiff as a piece of timber. I simply couldn't bend. I couldn't sit up, so three people lifted me like a board on their shoulders and carried me out of my "hole" to a borrowed station wagon. Sixty miles later, I was admitted to Deaconess Hospital in Wenatchee, Washington. It was the middle of summer, and I was not to return home until there was snow on the ground, 100 days later.

I remember there were two other polio patients admitted about the same time. One died the first week I arrived there. Another was Bette Wilder, a mother with two small children. Bette and I spent spent many, many hours together in therapy that year.

Polio delayed my dreams. Now I just wanted to relearn the simple tasks I had learned as a young child: feeding myself, dressing myself, standing and walking.

4

~~~

Physical Therapy 101 and Rehab 102

100 days in the hospital

Polio is a virus that blocks messages to the motor nerves. With no message, there is no movement. When the muscles don't get messages, they atrophy and cling to the good muscles. This, in turn, locks up the usable muscles and limits the range of motion.

At the hospital, I went through all the therapy known up to that time. I had daily whirlpool baths in butterfly-shaped Hubbard tanks, where therapists moved my limbs in a snow-angel pattern. I was also treated with hydrocollator steam packs, filled with silica gel, a variation of the hot, wet, wool packs made famous by pioneer polio nurse, Sister Kenny. Then there was the electrical muscular stimulation machine, which sent shocks through my muscles to force them to contract. Once the voltage was set too high and my leg jumped up from the table!

The worst part was the daily stretching. I vividly remember the pain. My legs were eventually pulled up over my head, to separate the atrophied muscles from

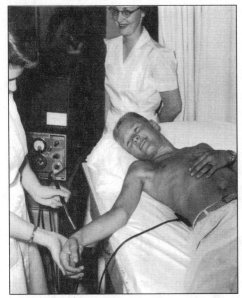

active ones to regain my range of motion. My wonderful, caring therapist, Carmen Bossenbrock, had a severe hearing loss and was kind enough to turn off her hearing aid and let me scream and yell during our stretching sessions. One day, my doctor came running into a therapy session, thinking someone was in dire need of help or surely dying. We

Carmen Bossenbrock using electrical muscular stimulation on Dan's right arm

stopped and laughed. It just felt good to yell!

It was several months before I stood up. Carmen strapped me to a tilt board hinged to a table top. Slowly they tilted the board to a 45-degree angle. They asked if I felt light-headed. "No problem," I said. We continued slowly toward upright. I then showed them how quickly I could pass out! It took several sessions before I could remain vertical, even while strapped to the tilt-table.

Because my paralyzed body did not respond very fast, I learned to focus on smaller goals. Carmen rigged rubber tubing overhead for me to pull down to work my left arm muscles. Often I would lose my grip and not be able to exercise until somebody replaced my hand on the tubing. One day, I realized I could "walk" the fingers of my left hand up my chest, and drag my arm up my neck to the top of my head. Then I would let my arm drop forward and, as it fell, grab the tubing. It wasn't much, but I did it by myself! It was the first of many small victories. There were setbacks, too—times I acutely realized that my life had been changed forever. One day I decided to walk. Carmen had warned me not to get out of bed, but I figured by locking my knees, I could stand up, then walk. I slowly slid off the side of the bed, grasping the sheets for support with my weak left hand. With my knees locked, I dropped to the floor. I attempted a step and promptly collapsed in a heap. Unfortunately, the call button was too short at one end so the floor became my final support until help arrived.

As soon as I could lift my left forearm, Carmen put a wooden dumbbell into my hand. It weighed an ounce! She had me lift that dumbbell until I could do ten repetitions. Then came the big one—two ounces. I called it "pumping wood"! Ultimately, I worked up to ten reps with eight pounds.

Once a week, I was taken to the Wenatchee YMCA heated swimming pool where I joined other polio survivors for therapy. Those were memorable trips. The ambulance crew would wrap me in towels in my bed, transfer me to a waterproof stretcher with bars on the sides, then carry me out to the ambulance for the five-block trip from the hospital to the Y. The driver would run the lights and sirens for me! At the Y, the towels were removed and a motorized hoist lowered my stretcher into the water. It was there that I learned to walk again with the help of rails put in neck-high water. After getting my body vertical, Carmen guided me through the motions of walking. As my legs became stronger, the rails were moved to shallower water, so I was bearing more body weight. When swim therapy time was over, I got the royal ride in the ambulance back to the hospital.

The pain and hard work were offset by reading stacks of cards and letters, some from people I didn't even know. Many said, "We are praying for your recovery." All were encouraging. A constant flow of visitors came through private room #118. We laughed, had fun, and pulled tricks on the nurses like pouring strong perfume in the bedpan. I was amazed how many people really cared for me.

Bette Wilder and I would get together at night and think of fun things to do. Once she wheeled into my room, knowing that Carmen would be checking on us soon. Carmen often stayed late, including this night when she dropped in around 10 p.m. We were ready for her. Neither Bette nor I smoked or gambled, but we had borrowed someone else's cigarettes and cards. We lit the cigarettes, smoked up the room, and were playing poker when Carmen walked in. We both laughed at the shocked look on Carmen's face.

It helped to have a sense of humor for some of those less pleasant necessities of life. Polio stagnated my elimination system. After trying unsuccessfully several times to get my bowels to move, I heard the doctor say, "That's it, we are going to blast." Then he ordered much stronger laxatives. I closed my eyes as they made me swallow the blasting caps. On the day of success, it seemed like the entire hospital celebrated. I learned that this is really a big deal in the hospital!

I did not like using a bedpan, so one of the male nurses would carry me to a bathroom down the hall. "Just whistle after you're finished," he said. I finished and dutifully whistled. Nobody heard me. I whistled and whistled. I then understood the meaning of "whistling in the wind."

After I was issued a wheelchair, life was never the same. I drove backwards using my left arm and right leg. I needed a rear-view mirror because I almost backed over several nurses! I was good at talking friends into providing the chairpower for my hospital explorations. Stopping the elevator between floors and getting ourselves into off-limits places occupied much of our time. I made friends in the cafeteria and would sneak down late at night for milk shakes. Sometimes visitors complained that they came to see this paralyzed guy and could never find him in bed!

My orthopedic doctor, Dr. Ed Cadman (later to become international president of Rotary Clubs), took special interest in me. Knowing I enjoyed sports, he would take me in my wheelchair to the Wenatchee Chiefs baseball games.

I never gave up on my dreams. Inch by inch, muscle by muscle, day by day, I kept working my way back, still thinking of college and other goals. Not only did I build up weakened muscles, at the same time I had to re-learn every skill over again as a one-armed, left-handed person. I returned to basic printing—after all, I would need to take notes in college. I spilled drinks and slopped food learning to eat. Ordinary skills were not ordinary at all. For example, to put on a pullover shirt, I had to use my teeth to hold it at the bottom of the back-side, so I could get my arms into it. I learned to tie shoes with one hand, do buttons with my mouth, and finally, walk with one Canadian forearm crutch. My weak left arm did all the work. I fell often, but knew where I was headed.

During September, I was given permission to be lifted into my parents' car for a little drive around town. At 25 miles per hour I was a nervous wreck. It seemed we were going at least 80! I had lost my perspective.

I was allowed to go home for a weekend, and went to the Okanogan County Fair. As my parents pushed me through the barns to see the animals and displays, I felt very self-conscious. People were staring at me. This was a whole new experience. I didn't like it. All I wanted to do was get out of that wheelchair, even though one doctor said I'd be sitting in it the rest of my life. I was determined to prove him wrong!

In early November, after I was able to walk fairly well on level ground with my crutch, I was released from the hospital. Carmen trained my sister, Marlene, and Mom to give me daily therapy. They set up a physical therapy exercise table with ropes and pulleys in the kitchen. We spent the next ten months in daily exercise and continued basic skill development

Polio was harder on my parents than it was on me. Although they were always supportive and encouraging, they never really shared their feelings. Soon after my release from the hospital, when I was barely able to get around, I was standing up with my crutch and for some reason said, "Look, I can run!" I whirled around and took one step, then my knees buckled and I hit the floor with a thud. My dad's emotional veneer cracked. He ran crying into his bedroom. That was when I really knew how much my illness had hurt them and their dreams for me. Years later, when I walked across the stage to get my master's degree, my mother-in-law told me, "Your dad turned to me and said, 'He isn't even limping!'"

Between exercise sessions, just sitting around became boring. To offset the boredom, Dad gave me his 35 mm camera to take black-and-white pictures. He set up a darkroom with a special chair so I could reach the enlarger and chemicals, and I spent many dark hours turning negatives into positives.

Because we lived close to the high school, the administrators agreed to let me come back and take a typing class. I ended up in a room full of old manual typewriters, now learning a left-handed typing technique. Basically I just taught myself the new skill. I didn't do badly either, scoring up to 44 words a minute without a mistake!

My legs were growing stronger, although I still needed my crutch. I started walking the two blocks to school for typing class. One day I decided to walk to the locker room and gym to soak up some good old athletic smells. Between the locker room and gym was a ramp. As I went up, I lost my balance and fell. I couldn't get up, and there was no one around to help me. A high school teacher soon came by, and we had a nice little chat. I think she was too embarrassed to ask if I needed help. I was embarrassed to ask her for assistance. I've noticed some people just do not know how to handle situations like this, so they avoid it, if they can. After she left, I was wondering how I would get up when a little sixth grader came along and asked, "Hey, you need help?" A sixth grader! Yup, he helped me up and I was on my way.

5

"Can I Give You a Lift?"

Survival in buildings with stairs

Icouldn't abandon my dreams; college was still a priority. In September, 1956, my reluctant parents drove me the 150 miles to Cheney, Washington, near Spokane, home of Eastern Washington College of Education. They moved me into a small first floor dormitory room in Hudson Hall, and left. I wonder now who was more scared.

Challenges loomed everywhere. This was long before laws mandated that public facilities be accessible to handicapped people.

Stairs made my life especially difficult. Some of my P.E. classes were sixteen impossible steps to the balcony level. Education classes were in Showalter Hall, a three-story building. I could barely walk with a crutch, let alone navigate steps. There was no way my left arm could pull me upstairs by the handrails.

I could not help but think of how the "old" Dan Miller would have bounded up those stairs three at a time. The new, "revised" me was stuck at the bottom of every stairwell. But thank goodness, not for long.

"Can I give you a lift?" somebody said behind me. I turned around and first laid eyes on Bruce Grambo, a football and track star. He grasped my hands, hoisted me to his back, and carried me up three flights of polished marble steps to my first education class. Before leaving, he said, "I'll meet you afterwards to get you back down." He kept his word.

Bruce introduced me to several other athletes who became my human elevators in various other buildings on campus.

One of my "carriers" was Ray Gilman, against whom I'd played basketball in high school. Ray and I enjoyed reliving the past competitive years. He was a good buddy who helped me survive that first year. Another good friend who helped me a great deal was Linden "Spike" Schuyler. He kept me laughing through the tough times.

The extent of challenges I faced getting around campus came back to me when my daughter Danica enrolled at my alma mater, now called Eastern Washington University. Her first month on campus, she wrote:

Dad, I have just begun to really appreciate your sense of determination. There are several disabled people up here who have a super hard time getting around—wheelchairs, crutches, braces, etc. I am so glad and proud of you that you went through all that pain and torture to become the great administrator you are. I think I have it rough, walking all over, up hills and so on, but you, dear old Dad, have all my condolences for all your hard work. I never realized how hard it must have been on you. I hope I will have that much determination. Thanks. By the way, if I do decide to graduate, I will probably go into education. I really enjoy that class. Who knows?

Danica not only survived the hills and all the walking, she persevered, became a teacher and obtained a master's degree in education.

6

~~~

My Idea of Exercise Is a Good Brisk Sit

The dream in action: P.E. activity classes

My P.E. major required me to pass eleven activity classes. Some were easier than others. Weight lifting and swimming helped me gain more strength, but I really enjoyed my class of trampoline skills. That contraption set me free! With one leg locked, I could jump, land, and actually jump again—something I hadn't been able to do since polio. How I savored that freedom.

My P.E. professor, Dr. Glen Kirchner, said he would grade me separately from other students, because of my handicap. At the end of the trampoline class, I received an "A," but it was a very special "A." He placed me into the regular class grading curve after all, because I excelled. I could do rolls and flips and invented a few moves with some twists I didn't realize I could do!

I also became quite proficient at one sport that was not in the P.E. catalog. While I was at home rehabilitating, my dad set up a Ping-Pong table and a special chair for me to sit in. It was good exercise for my left arm and gave me something more to do with my sisters and friends. By the time I entered college I was able to stand and play, and became one of the best Ping-Pong players in the dorm. I always tried to play with my legs locked, but every once in a while when reaching too far for a ball, my legs would unlock and I would collapse and disappear under the table. Through Ping-Pong I made a lot of friends. It felt good to compete again.

As I worked my part-time job in the athletic department, the competitive juices flowed when I saw athletes practicing rebounds, jump shots and free throws. I couldn't jump any more. I was still right-handed in my mind. I wanted to shoot baskets again. For a while I couldn't lift a basketball, let alone shoot it. I tried shooting a lighter weight ball, but every time it fell miserably short. One day I figured out that if I twisted my body like a shot-putter, turned, twisted and threw my arm and the ball, I could get more power in my shot. It worked, but my accuracy was terrible. It took three weeks before I finally scored. I persisted, however, and slowly began to control that crazy shot. A year later I was able to handle a volleyball, then later, had enough strength to shoot a real basketball. I became deadly within twelve feet of the basket, but was still too weak for the long shots. Shooting games of "Around the World" and "H-O-R-S-E" were now my areas of expertise.

Years later, when I was teaching P.E. and coaching student athletes for the Elks' State Hoop Shoot contest, I made 96 of 100 free throws with that crazy, improvised left-handed shot!

7

~~~~~

From "Crippled" to "Mobility Impaired"

Self-esteem and "politically correct" labels

It's interesting how our *politically correct* terms change. In the '50s they called me *crippled*. By the '60s I was *handicapped*. In the '70s the term was *disabled*. Then, in the '80s, I was *physically challenged*. Now, in the '90s, I'm *mobility impaired*. I wonder what I will be next?

One day I was under a trampoline, struggling to hook it together. A student came in and asked another student, "Where is that little crippled boy who works around here?" Suddenly, I realized he was talking about me. I stayed hidden, trying to ignore his thoughtless remark.

People stared, but I had learned to accept my body and ignore their stares. When others made fun of me or my physical limitations, I decided they were the ones who were limited, not me. I realized my friends and family loved me because of who I was and how I treated them, not on the basis of what I looked like. I still liked myself and believed I was special and important. I accepted myself just the way I was, and those who were my true friends looked past my ugly arm and legs. In part, because of them, I could stand in front of my mirror each morning and say, "Dan, you're an awesome dude." I focused on what I could do, not on what I couldn't do!

Something, however, had to be done with my useless right arm. One thing that helped was surgery between my college freshman and sophomore years. In what was a fairly new operation at that time, Dr. Ed Cadman fused my right wrist to increase power to squeeze and hold with my fingers. He neglected to tell me he would use a piece of my hip to do this. I had just gotten to the point in my rehabilitation where I was able to walk fairly well, then after my wrist fusion, I couldn't walk again until my hip healed!

Another operation transplanted my right forearm finger flexor muscles to act as substitute biceps. Prior to that surgery, lifting my arm was impossible because my biceps were atrophied. Afterwards, squeezing my fingers pulled my forearm upward a few inches. That meant I was using those flexor muscles at both ends. Dr. Cadman was quite proud of the results and showed off my repaired arm to other doctors.

However, I was not the model patient. After the transplant surgery, my arm was in a huge cast bent at a severe angle toward my chin. Because it was summer and hot, the lake looked awfully good. My cousin Elden Stennes and I decided to do a little boating at Alta Lake. Unfortunately, a wave from another boat swamped us and our boat filled with water. Elden fell over the side, but I hung on and stayed with the boat. Elden didn't know that. He thought I had gone under water with a huge cast that was as good as a millstone for sending me to the bottom. He kept diving under the boat, looking for me, finally realizing I was hanging on to the boat. Somebody towed us to shore, and as soon as we reached the dock, the boat sank. I had to get a new cast, but it was worth it for the fun and sense of freedom that boating gave me!

8

There is No Problem So Great, I Can't Ignore

Wrist action, finger movement and guitar pickin´

My first guitar was under the Christmas tree in 1951. It was a Harmony brand which came from a "Monkey" Ward catalog.

My mom played piano, and I learned a little piano by ear, but the guitar was for me. My favorite singer /songwriter /musician was Hank Williams. I plunked away and learned to chord to "Hey, Good Lookin'," "Jambalaya" and "Lovesick Blues."

When we moved from Mansfield to Pateros in 1953, I met Perry Buster who was an excellent singer and guitar player. By then I could play chords pretty well, so we teamed up and played, dreaming of the day we would have our own band.

Perry was also my teammate in sports. Of the five boys in our class, only Perry and I turned out for sports.

After polio, I wondered if my guitar-playing days were over. I couldn't raise my hands above my shoulders, so getting a guitar strapped on was a bit of a challenge. I had enough strength in my left hand to finger the chords, but couldn't strum with my right hand. My thumb wouldn't budge, my fingers wouldn't open, my wrist was fused and my arm wouldn't straighten out. No one believed I would ever play again. I kept trying, but nothing seemed to work.

Then in my sophomore year of college, cousin Elden, my boating partner, was killed in a devastating car accident. My uncle asked if I wanted Elden's bass guitar. He had just purchased one of the first Fender Precision electric bass guitars ever made. I said, "Yes!" Its strings were larger and spaced further apart. My left hand could manage that a little better, but I still had a strumming problem until I realized I could rest the thumb of my right hand where the guitar neck met the body. I found I could strum using two fingers without moving my arm. And I had sound, especially with an amplifier!

Elden's amplifier was too small for a band, so my buddy Perry and I bought an old Wurlitzer jukebox, tore out the amplifier and 15-inch speaker, and made a bass amplifier for about $45. We were in business! Perry and I rounded up a couple of other musicians and formed our band. I sang harmony and the bass became my instrument. Perry sang the lead, and played guitar. Merlin Cannell also sang, and played lead guitar. Jerry Robison manned the drums. We called ourselves *The Stompers* and played all over the Northwest, with engagements in Washington, Idaho, Montana, and British Columbia. We played locally at Plaza Grange Hall and the E.W.S.C. campus. Every engagement put a little more in our college bank accounts. Our band stayed together from 1958 to 1964. (Bob Dunkin stepped in for Perry while he served in the Army.) In 1959 we made a record in Coeur d'Alene, Idaho, and won the *Battle of the Bands* competition against ten other Northwest bands.

Ah, the stories that Fender Precision Bass Guitar and

*The "Stompers"—Dan, Merlin Cannell,
Jerry Robinson, and Perry Buster*

I could tell about the Stompers' adventures, but I will pass and let Perry share one:

We were hired by a rock and roll radio station in Butte, Montana, to play a New Year's Eve dance for teens. After driving all day from Spokane to Butte, playing penny ante poker most of the way, we set up to face 1,100 excited teenagers (live rock music bands were very rare back then). When the promoters brought out the free horns and hats at midnight, they plunked them on the stage. We were ambushed and almost trampled as we tried to protect our equipment and ourselves. We were paid 500 silver dollars (Butte used silver dollars exclusively in those days) and walked out to the car lugging bags of money.

Judy and I didn't have much money at that time and vividly remember pouring our share of 100-plus silver dollars on the apartment floor and running barefoot through them! I will let Perry finish:

The next day we were to play a high school dance in Deer Lodge, Montana. The school board cancelled it because they didn't like some of the songs that our sponsoring radio station was playing. We heard that there was a record dance down the road in Anaconda, so we dropped by and talked them into letting us play "live" music. I guess they thought we were big stars because we signed all kinds of autographs, even on girls' arms!

The next morning we started the long drive home, knowing we were low on gas. We thought we could stretch it to Wallace, Idaho. We had to go over 4,700-foot Lookout Pass and just a few hundred feet from the summit, our gas ran out. Suddenly, some skiers threw down their skis and ran towards us yelling, "The Stompers, it's the Stompers!" They were fans from our own college. We put Dan behind the wheel and we all pushed that heavy four-door '57 Mercury up to the top. Dan put it into neutral, and we coasted down the mountain for thirteen miles and right into a gas station. Dan actually passed two cars and a semi-truck and trailer on the way down. Other than that it was an uneventful trip.

I didn't play a six-string guitar with the Stompers, but I kept fooling around with one trying to learn how to play chords. When I started teaching sixth grade, I knew the students would love to sing with me playing the guitar. I kept working at it, and we had some sing-alongs at camp. I found that singing brings happiness and joy, so as a P.E. teacher and later as a principal, I often played my guitar. I had several sing-alongs every year for my staff and students. It was a joy to sing and play the guitar, not only at school, but with my own kids as they were growing up, and then at church. Now I play and sing for my grand-kids, making singing tapes for them from their "Papa."

9

The Best Way to Get a Healthy Body Is to Marry One

Romancing Judy

I never gave up my dream of someday marrying a beautiful girl and having outstanding kids. In high school, I tended to focus on sports more than girls. I was not the big-time ladies' guy, though I did have a girl friend my senior year of high school. When I would date a new girl, I would take Bonnie, my fifth grade sister, with us. She would sit between me and my date. We would laugh and have a great time, but those girls didn't seem to like threesomes. By the time I was a college sophomore, I had gone on a few dates, but had not met anyone special. Then one day something happened in the college cafeteria. I'll let Judy tell the story:

He was walking—limping, really—past me with his meal tray in the dining hall. He was wearing a light tan car coat with pants that were rolled up a couple of notches. I remember thinking he was kind of cute and that he must be a farm boy, used to rolling his pants up to keep them out of the manure.

He looked over and said "hello" to the person I was eating with and hobbled off. I remember he had a nice smile and twinkling eyes, but I was used to dating big guys and he was really little in comparison. In fact, I then had a boyfriend who was a football player at the University of Washington. I never thought about dating Dan. He was just passing through while we were eating. Naturally the conversation turned toward him.

"That's Danny Miller," my eating companion said. "He was offered a basketball scholarship to several colleges but ended up with polio the summer he graduated from high school."

I figured that's why he walked so funny. The next time I saw Dan, he was walking up and down the long line of people waiting to get into the dining hall. He would speak briefly to someone, then move on. I soon found out he was looking for someone who knew me, so he could be formally introduced. Finally, he pulled someone out from the line and they both came toward me. The person performed a quick introduction and left. Since there is not much to do while waiting in line, this little scene was followed closely by everyone. I was surprised, embarrassed, and a little flattered. Dan was oblivious to everyone but me.

I figured since we had been introduced, it was okay to call Judy for a date. I asked her to go have a soda at the Student Union building. She said, "YES!" I was so excited I tripped and fell on the way. She picked me up and we laughed and started to get acquainted that day. Of course, I had competition from her football-player boyfriend at another college. He came one weekend to see her, and when he found out about me, he remarked, "He's crippled!" Judy replied, "He is not crippled when you get to know him."

I remember the first time Judy took me home to meet her mother. For dinner, her mother served steak. As I struggled to cut it with my weak left hand, both steak and plate zoomed to the floor and whirled around, dumping food all over the rug. Some impression I must have made on her mom!

Judy picks up our story again:

Judy and Dan, dating in College

Dan and I often went to the library to study. After all, we were at college to get an education. Dan didn't need to study as long or as much as I did. He would wait for me to finish so we could leave together. If I took too long, he would take drastic measures. They usually consisted of ways to get me laughing. This was pretty easy to do, especially when he used his loud swallowing technique. Once I began laughing, he would join in and soon the librarian would ask us to leave. How can you study after you leave the library?

Since we both took biology, we studied together for that final until we reached the hows and whats of human reproduction. Dan suggested we study that separately. In those days we didn't say "sex" out loud, or name body parts in mixed company. Maybe it was better that way.

Then again, some aspects of the boy-girl scene in the late '50s need to remain buried in history. At that time, the girls were locked in their dorms after curfew, presumably to keep them safe from college boys. One time my buddy Perry and I safely returned Judy to her dorm, then jumped into our jalopy for the traditional "good night" cruise around the girls' building.

Our jalopy was virtually our trademark. We named it *Grozma* (we wanted a special name, one that wasn't even in the dictionary.) Everybody recognized this crazy old Model A coupe with its top cut off to make it a cool convertible. We joined the parade of guys driving around the dorm, honking and waving to the locked-up girls, who hung out their windows and waved and hollered at us.

Perry was driving, and as he approached the corner of that little dirt road, he decided to hit the throttle, spin the wheels and slide around the corner to impress the girls, especially Judy. His door flew open and he fell out, leaving me in the passenger seat of this still-moving vehicle! It surprised him, entertained the girls, and

scared me spitless. I was able to reach over with my foot and hit the brake before the car went off the road. Perry jumped up out of the dirt, dusted himself

Perry Buster, Dan and "Grozma"

off, and climbed back into *Grozma* for a red-faced exit.

10

〜〜

Marry Me and I'll Never Bother You Again

Real living and loving

Judy and I had been dating about a year when I decided I would ask her to marry me. I went to Spokane and chose a ring. Later, I picked her up and we drove to a dark, quiet spot outside of town and parked. "I saw some chocolate-covered ants in Spokane," I told Judy, asking her to hold out her hand. She thought I was going to put chocolate ants in her hand. What I really had was *the ring*! She reacted by flinging up her hand, and the ring went flying through my dark car. We had to search the car, find the ring, then go outside and use the headlights so she could see what she perhaps would be wearing for the rest of her life.

Here is more from Judy:

On August 15, 1959, I married that man. To this day, he continually surprises me with his approach to the world and

Dan and Judy, August 15, 1959

people in it. He brings joy and happiness to our lives and a richness that I could never have imagined. He is still cute and has that twinkle in his eyes. He has never been a little man. He is a giant!

We didn't own a dependable car, so my friend Bruce Grambo loaned us his hot rod for our honeymoon trip. It was a '39 chopped and channeled Ford convertible. It also had a Chrysler "Hemi" V8-supercharged racing engine. When we took off from the church, we left black streaks for a block down Main Street, Pateros. Our local police officer, Roy Gebbers, just covered his eyes, laughed, and let us go. He could not have caught us anyway!

Here's some more from Judy:

Our first home was an upstairs apartment that rented for $30 a month. This was a bargain since it was across the street from campus, which made walking to classes easy. We did not have a driveable car for much of our first year. The most outstanding feature of this apartment was the smell. The downstairs neighbors were not very clean people. Actually, they were slobs. They piled their garbage in the hallway. We would take a deep breath before opening the door, and run up the stairs to our door. Dan was slow up the stairs but he could hold his *breath longer. The trick was to make it up the stairs and in the door before we had to take a breath. Sometimes we were successful.*

Our first (and last) fight, and my embarrassing outburst, happened one night when we were getting ready to go to the movies. Dan is very, very slooow. I am very, very speedy. We were running a little late. I was walking behind him through the front room. I was giving him an important running commentary on the time situation and probably suggesting that he might move faster. He responded by picking up his right arm with his left and placing his index finger in his right ear. With that finger in place, he proceeded to insert his left index finger in his left ear as he continued to sloooowly amble toward the door. That did it. I pulled back my arm and planted my fist with a resounding thud right between his shoulder blades. There was a sound of air escaping through his mouth, but he said nothing as he kept walking to the door. I was absolutely shocked that I would do such a thing. I can't remember anything else—except it has never happened again.

I graduated with a Bachelor of Arts in Education the following June and took a job teaching sixth grade at Fairchild Air Force Base in the Medical Lake School District. My first contract was for $4,150 a year. My take-home pay was $288 a month. We decided to move into Spokane and actually bought a little house for $79 a month.

Though we had been married a year, we looked like teenagers. One evening after we moved in, the coal furnace acted up. Judy called her grandma to ask what to do. Grandma told Judy to call the fire department, and they would send a person out to check on it. A few minutes later, here came a huge fire truck, sirens howling and lights flashing. It stopped in front of our house and several firemen in full fire gear came streaming through our door and into our basement. They found the furnace needed the clinkers cleaned out. As we stood there in shock, I remember the head fireman asking us if our parents were home. I said "no" and left it at that!

After two years in Spokane, we moved to Coulee Dam. I taught sixth grade and earned an additional $200 a year for coaching basketball, football and softball. We rented a small house for $47.50 a month. Judy painted it inside and out in exchange for the first month's rent.

One of life's necessities was a washer, and we got our first at a yard sale for $5. It was a bolt-down automatic Bendix. One day Judy went down to the basement and found it walking all over the place! The bolts had worked loose. Panicked, she lay across it until it quit. She kept it in place, but turning it off might have been wiser as she was eight months pregnant at the time! During those first few years of marriage Judy and I put our biology class notes to good work. We had three babies in four and a half years.

After four years of teaching sixth grade, I decided I needed my master's degree, so I quit my Coulee Dam job and moved back to Eastern Washington, now a University. We rented a house, signed up for summer classes, and then went job-hunting. I had planned to make some money playing in a band with my buddy Perry, but that didn't work out. An educational grant was available, but a mix-up reported my grade point wrong, so I was denied that money. Here I was, two quarters from my master's degree, a wife and three babies to support, and no job.

I went into Spokane and applied as a substitute teacher. They needed someone to fill in for a fifth grade teacher who had a recent heart attack, so I took that position from the time school started until Christmas vacation. They wanted me to stay on, but I knew I had to get back to my master's degree. Judy did her student teaching during that time. She taught high school home economics and first grade. At the same time, she took two night classes and a correspondence course—26 credits hours in all—while being mom to three little kids.

Three weeks into her student teaching she was hired to teach full time starting in January, and I went back to graduate school. Karmen was six months old, Danica was two and a half, and Sky was four. We drove 70 miles a day taking kids to babysitters and getting to our schools. Somehow we got through that year!

We had signed a one-year lease on a house which expired June 30. The landlords lived in Oregon. They didn't plan to move back. Then, they informed us we had to be out June 1. Since I didn't graduate until June 15 and Judy was still teaching, we had no choice but to move into a motel for two weeks. We moved as I was finishing my studies, interviewing for P.E. teaching jobs, and Judy was finishing her teaching year. Sky, our eldest child, became very ill with severe asthma during this busy time. *We were _not_ having fun.*

Two weeks later, we moved again, this time back to my parent's home in Pateros. I had the master's degree, but no job, and no money. We slept under the stars in Mom and Dad's apple orchard that summer. I'm sure my mom and dad wondered what good that master's degree was but they never said a critical word about our dilemma. They just accepted and supported us.

Most teachers were already hired for the next year, but I was still turning down job offers. I contacted 55 school districts from Las Vegas to Nome in person or by phone. I turned down at least twenty offers to be a classroom teacher, because I really had my heart set on teaching P.E. I had been dreaming of a P.E. position for several years. Near mid-summer I learned of a P.E specialist opening in Bellingham, Washington. This was not just a teaching job, it was supervisor of elementary P.E. for 160 teachers in 15 elementary schools! This was a goal of mine, but I thought I needed several years more experience for this one. Still, I applied, and landed that job over many able-bodied candidates. The Bellingham position was the only elementary P.E. job opening in the Northwest that year. If I had signed any of the classroom-teaching offers, I would not have been available to take that wonderful dream-job. Sometimes persistence and even a little stubbornness pays off!

In August, we loaded up our three little kids, stacked all our possessions in my dad's cattle truck, and headed over the mountains to a place we knew nothing about.

11

When All Else Fails, Lower Your Standards

"Woody," the almost-live teaching dummy

At Bellingham, my handicap became a problem in demonstrating P.E. skills. I would tell kids to put out their hands to catch a ball, but I could only demonstrate with my left hand while my right hand stayed limp at my side. The kids would copy me, reaching out with just one hand.

I soon bought an assistant: an 18-inch wooden art mannequin which demonstrated what I wanted students to do. The mannequin easily showed positions for pushups, catching and other skills. I discovered it could also stand on its head. From there, other ideas started flowing. I named this doll "Woody" and kids quickly bonded with him. I used Woody for almost every lesson. When I came in for that school's weekly lesson, I would tell a story about Woody.

I might say Woody was hit on his nose when he tried to catch a ball because he didn't have his hands up in the right position. I would put Woody's hands up and say, "This is how Woody now gets ready to catch a ball. Can you do that?" Judy made little jump ropes and rice-filled beanbags for him. The kids really focused on Woody and sometimes he would get a laugh, making it all the more fun for them to learn.

Little by little, Woody's pile of sports gear and clothes grew. Judy made him little hats, pants, and shirts. He even had a University of Washington shirt and football helmet! One time I found a miniature raft and brought it to school to tell the kids that Woody rafted the river that summer. We found some things for him at crafts stores plus kids would bring him toys. A lot of clever things—even a beach umbrella—came when the teachers gave Woody a shower. We accumulated so much that I filled a briefcase just with *Woody's Goodies*. Woody became so well-known that I even displayed him at open house. Parents would come up and say, "This is Woody? From the way the kids talked about him, I imagined him six feet tall." In their minds, Woody was real. They identified with his character. That's when Woody went beyond his P.E. duties. I started sending students Christmas letters from Woody. Even years later when I became a principal, Woody became my Assistant Principal. I'd have Woody "write" to the incoming kindergartners. They could hardly wait to start school and meet him. In my bulletins, I had Woody tell how he got hit in the face with a snowball, and it really hurt. Woody didn't have a face; that made him more intriguing.

Before long I gave Woody a voice. I played my guitar and sang into a sound-on-sound tape recorder. Then I would speed it up, Chipmunk-style, so Woody had his own voice. Woody and I both talked and laughed and sang to the students. Judy made him a little Santa outfit and bought him a little guitar. At Christmas time, Woody and I teamed up with duets, singing "Jingle Bells," "Rudolph," and "Away in a Manger."

During the school year we performed half-hour sing-alongs with each class. The kids would love it when Woody would get mixed up and sing, "Mommas, Don't Let Your Cowboys Grow Up to Be Babies!". Woody was almost human to them. Even now when I run into former students who are in college or parents themselves, they will ask me, "Do you still have

Dan and Woody singing at a school Christmas program

Woody?" When my daughter went to her ten-year high school reunion, they all wanted to know how Woody was. One young man, when he was a junior in college, visited me and asked to see all of Woody's gear. When I used the mannequin in school I never showed everything in his briefcase. I would pick a student to come up and choose two things from the case to show everyone, and then I would close the cover. So the briefcase's entire contents remained a mystery. I suppose some are still wondering what they missed of *Woody's Goodies!*

12

If Your Parents Didn't Have Children, Chances Are You Won't Either

Accepting kids just the way they are

Sometimes people look at us and our kids and think we have it all together and never had problems. One time I spoke to a group of parents whose children's problems were targeted by a federal program. The leader did not want me to show pictures of our children, thinking her group couldn't relate to blond, blue-eyed kids who seemed healthy and successful in every way. Judy told her, "This family did not just happen. We spent a lot of time making it a success. We have had health problems. We were poor, trying to live on one teacher's salary while I stayed home with the kids. We ate lots of macaroni and cheese." I went ahead and showed our family pictures and mentioned our kids' health problems. Seeing how well her group responded to our real story, the leader later apologized.

The real story is that Sky developed asthma as an infant. He was in the hospital off and on several times during the first years of his life, struggling to breathe under an oxygen tent. For the first twelve years of his life he woke up every night, coughing and choking with asthma. Judy got up every night with him. It was rugged! Recently doctors determined that he has only 40 to 50% of normal lung capacity, but Sky has lived with his asthma so long that he doesn't think of himself as having a big problem.

When Danica was about four years old we discovered she had epilepsy. She experienced petit mal seizures.

Danica, Karmen, and Sky

She'd just "check out" for a short time. We knew something was wrong when one evening, after we finished giving thanks for our food, Danica spoke up and said, "Aren't we going to say the blessing?" She had a petit mal seizure during the blessing. She was on medication for that until she was a teenager.

Then when Danica and Karmen were in pre-school we learned their "fat necks" were the result of goiters. Both started on thyroid medicine they would take the rest of their lives. As an adult Karmen had half of her thyroid removed. In addition, Karmen had a bleeding factor related to hemophilia.

Perhaps because I had learned to live with my handicap from polio, we decided not to shelter and limit our children. After Danica was diagnosed with epilepsy, the doctor advised us not to let her ride a bike, but Judy and I felt it was more important to let her have as normal a childhood as possible. We had little Honda motorcycles for the kids and we allowed her to ride one of those, but she had to have someone watching. The same with Sky. It would have been easy to overprotect him. When he was out in the cold air and started running, he became miserable with spells of coughing and gagging. Sometimes when the kids were in the yard tossing a football around, Sky sat on the sidelines fighting for every breath. The doctor said Sky's asthma problem was a long-term thing. His personality development was more important to us than protecting him from his physical problems. We encouraged him to try things. He needed to monitor himself.

Our children grew up accepting and living beyond their health problems because that's the way they saw me live. I didn't post any "keep off" signs on me! When we would get down on the floor to wrestle, they would say, "Go for Dad's arm." They knew if they grabbed my left arm and sat on it, they would keep me from grabbing them or getting away. It only took one kid sitting on my left arm for me to yell "uncle"!

When Sky was 2 1/2, Judy noticed he had a peculiar way of running and feared he had a leg problem. The doctor found nothing physically wrong with him. A few days later Judy looked out the window to see Sky and me chasing each other. We both "ran" (limped) the same way. Like father, like son! It was time for Mom to give some running lessons to her son!

Our family, 1968

Danica was six when she first heard her dad was "crippled." I was telling at dinner how I had gone to the newspaper office to pick up a paper being held for me. The man at the counter told me they were all gone. "But I asked to have one reserved," I insisted. The counter man yelled to the back room, "This guy says you were holding a paper for him." The back room voice replied,

"I've got one for a crippled guy." "That would be me," I said.

Danica's head popped up from eating. "Crippled?" she asked. "Who's crippled?" Judy took this "teachable moment" to explain that I was crippled. Danica looked at me and said, "Oh, yuck! A crippled dad." And then she went back to her meal.

Karmen says she was in seventh grade before she realized her dad was "handicapped." She had picked up the mail on her way up the driveway and noticed a letter to "Handicapped Person" at our address. She asked Judy why somebody would send us such a letter since we didn't have handicapped people at our house. When Judy explained that I was considered "handicapped," Karmen says she filed that away for future reference. Recently Karmen remarked:

I thought everybody's mom fixed the bike tires or did carpentry around the house. Dad's paralysis was never an issue. If anything, we got special privileges for being the P.E. teacher's children. We could stay after school to bounce on the trampoline, shoot baskets, or walk on the balance beam. Sometimes he would pull us out of class to demonstrate something on the trampoline for other classes. We felt so important!

13

The Fall and Rise of Dan Miller

Memorable falls

They say one of the things an ice skater needs to learn very well is how to fall. Well, that's really true of anybody whose legs are 80 per cent paralyzed. I have fallen so many times I should write this great book titled *The Fall and Rise of Dan Miller.*

I fell repeatedly in the hospital when I was trying my hardest to learn to walk again. After I left the hospital, I used one Canadian (forearm) crutch because only my left arm was strong enough to hold it. It wasn't great stability, but it was all I had. Getting up after falling was impossible, but I learned to make the best of my perspective—especially the "looking up" one.

One snowy November day, just after my release from the hospital, my dad took me along while he did some errands in town. When we got home, he helped me out of the car, stood me up in about six inches of snow, and asked me to wait while he carried the groceries up the front steps. Before he got back, I lost my balance and fell backwards into the snow. When he returned I was having a great time, making snow angels.

While at college, I was a little steadier on my feet, but I still fell a half dozen times a day. Some students came along and picked me up. Other students, not sure what to say or do, just walked around me as I struggled to get up.

Once I fell in front of the Student Union Building on my way to class. I had a briefcase hooked to my crutch and as I fell, it flipped under me and I landed on it, breaking it open. All my papers spewed out. I was so angry about breaking my briefcase that I just sat there. Eventually somebody helped me up and life went on.

Falling took on another dimension when I got married and had kids. When Karmen was six, we were at the old J.J. Newberry store in Spokane. She ran up to me, grabbed me at knee level, and down we went, me on top of her in the middle of two intersecting aisles. My left arm was pinned under Karmen and she was under me! No matter how much we struggled, we couldn't get up. A stunned and staring crowd gathered but, surprisingly, offered no help. All Karmen and I could do was lay there and laugh. Finally, Judy heard the commotion and came to our rescue.

Probably the granddaddy of all my falls came when I lived in Leavenworth, right at the edge of the Cascade Mountains. It was a perfect place for great snow-falls. I slipped on some snow, and fell forward, uphill. My left leg went forward and my right leg backward with my chest on top of my left leg. It tore several muscles in my hamstring area. My whole leg turned black and blue and my knee started clicking and clacking, popping and locking up, whenever I walked. An orthopedic doctor advised surgery before it locked up completely. I kept putting it off. A few weeks later I endured another nasty fall and twisted my knee—but that seemed to fix it! It swelled and needed to be drained, but never again clicked and clacked or gave me problems. Sometimes taking a fall can turn out to be a blessing. Other times, not.

Another winter day at Leavenworth, as I walked to the bus garage, a snow-covered patch of ice threw my feet into the air, and dropped me hard onto my back. It knocked the breath out of me and cracked several ribs under my left arm. The pain made life almost unbearable. I was nearly incapacitated, but the fall reminded me of how life might have been if I hadn't regained use of some of my muscles. My left arm helps me sit up, get up out of bed and out of a chair. Judy had to help me out of bed and dress me. While doing this, we got the giggles. It hurt so much to laugh, I made her leave the room. She did, but couldn't stop laughing. I would hear her, and burst into laughter and howl in pain simultaneously. How we stopped, I can't remember.

It was after this painful incident that I finally swallowed my pride and ordered a handicapped parking sticker.

Considering all the things I've done and risked, I've been very fortunate. One time I was riding a motorcycle in the Horse Heaven Hills in southeast Washington with a friend, Wendy Weld. My Honda 70 trail bike's front wheel dropped into a gopher hole, and the bike and I went tumbling end over end down the steep hill. Wendy said it was spectacular! If I had broken my left arm, I would have again been helpless. Fortunately, I didn't.

One day we took our family skiing with our friends, the Lyons. I had every intention of curling up in the lodge with cocoa and a good book, letting the others ski. Nothing doing! My friend Lois coerced me into trying downhill skiing. They strapped these huge ski boots and skis on me. Our kids locked their arms around me, held me up, and our group went up the rope tow. Somehow they got me up the rope tow and pointed me down the hill. I locked my legs and away I went. There was more pressure on the right ski, so that turned me continually left. I shot down the hill in an arc for nearly 100 yards, then fell and rolled quite a ways before I could stop. I had to twist, roll, and flip over to face the opposite direction. Then, after figuring out how to get up, I repeated the procedure, down the entire hill.

I've had my share of falls on the golf course too. In 1996 I was playing with my son, Sky. We both hit onto the green. Grabbing my putter, I started down a muddy slope. I slipped, both legs buckled, and down I went, head first this time. I dug a muddy divot with my nose and chin, managed to get my nose out of the mud, but couldn't get up, having pinned my putter and left arm underneath my body. Sky had seen me fall many times, but this time when he noticed I didn't get up right away he said, "Hey, Dad, are you all right?"

I looked up from the mud and shot back, "Of course, I'm just lining up my putt!" We laughed and he picked me up. I made the putt!

By now Judy is used to my falling. Several times I have offered to help her walk when it was slippery (that is gentlemanly, you know), but I ended up falling and pulling her down with me!

We keep this saying on our office wall:
I said, "Lean on me."
She did, and we both fell!

14

~~~

If It's Worth Doing, It's Worth Doing Poorly at First

Dan's first flying lesson

As I settled into my education career, I realized how many of my dreams had come true. I had finished college, married a lovely lady, had three beautiful children, and was teaching P.E. I had learned to play the guitar, the bass, and had performed for eight years in a band, moonlighting for extra income.

However, there was still one unfulfilled dream. My heart did little leaps every time I saw a plane overhead. I hung around airports and talked to people about flying, but they would take one look at me and remind me that airplanes were not like cars with power steering and automatic transmissions. Planes required two good hands and two good legs to work the controls, yokes, radio, and rudder pedals. "Airplanes crash," they would say. "You'll kill yourself." "You only have one good arm."

"Your legs are too weak." I heard a lot of *Dream-breaker* statements.

We'd moved in 1968 to Prosser, Washington, where I taught P.E. for ten years before becoming an elementary principal. One day near the local airport, I almost drove off the road while gawking at a plane taking off. Judy said, "Go out there and take a lesson, Dan." She knew I still had that dream.

Judy and Dan 1968

There was an auction in town and the Thompson Flight School offered a gift certificate for a 30-minute introductory flight lesson. I bought it. On May 26, 1975, I took my first lesson with Cormac Thompson Sr., a 68-year-old veteran pilot, licensed in 1929.

Normally, student pilots sit in the left seat of the airplane. I am sure Mr. Thompson wondered what he had gotten into as I figured out how to get my paralyzed body up into the low-wing Cherokee 140. Normally, you mount a step and walk up the wing to the door. Not being able to do that, I did my two-knee, one-hand crawl up the wing, then worked my way into the left seat of the four-cylinder Piper.

Mr. Thompson gave me a brief overview of the switches and controls and allowed me to taxi the plane to the end of runway 25. Right away I knew this was not like driving a car. I tried to "steer" with the "steering wheel" and learned this contraption (called the "yoke") wasn't connected to the wheels. Instead, the rudder pedals turned the plane.

We went through the run-up checklist and pulled onto the runway for takeoff. Wow! He had me push the throttle all the way in, and in a few seconds we had an airspeed of 60 MPH. His hands and feet were on the right side controls. I followed his lead.

"Let's rotate," he said.

"What?" I asked, dizzy with the thrill of takeoff.

"Pull back on the yoke." As I eased back on the wheel, er, yoke, the plane soared into the air and we were flying! He flew us to a practice area, then turned the controls over to me. It was awful! I had to reach across my body for the flaps, throttle, and trim. Every time I'd reach for them, the plane would dip, tip, and do everything but fly straight and level. I went all over the sky. I couldn't fly. After we landed, I realized my lesson was a failure. But I couldn't give up yet.

15

Who Says Turkeys Can't Fly?

The dream comes true

I was disappointed with my first flying lesson, but I had an idea. I went back to the airport and suggested we try again with me in the right-hand seat. That way I could access the controls better with my left hand. Mr. Thompson agreed. The next try, though not good, was better. I tell people, *"If it's worth doing, it's worth doing poorly at first!"* After that, we flew once or twice a week in a Piper Cherokee, call letters 4258 Juliet.

Many people would have had me stop after that first lesson. When my grandma heard I was learning to fly, she remarked, "Mercy, you only have one good arm and the hills are already full of little Cessnas!" But I wasn't listening to Grandma. I was listening to Judy, my dreammaker. She believed I could do it. Flying required adjustments for my "limitations." From the right-hand seat I was reading instruments from across the cockpit making mental adjustments for the angle in reading the airspeed, altitude and climb rate.

Most pilots keep one hand on the throttle at all times while taking off and landing. Several throttle adjustments are needed as varying wind conditions cause the plane to balloon or sink. This is especially critical during approach before landing. Adjusting the throttle helps maintain the desired altitude.

I had to learn to adjust the throttle to the exact setting I wanted, and get my hand back quickly to the yoke for control of pitch and roll. I also had to quickly adjust the trim (to take pressure off the yoke) and the flaps (to slow the plane for landing). During the landing sequence, while busily trying to keep the plane level, slowing it down, putting down flaps, reducing throttle, and adjusting trim several times, I was asked to pick up the microphone and announce my position and intentions to other aircraft in the area. At first this was too much to handle.

I also had to learn a new language which I call Pilot Talk. In a calm, audible voice (while sweating profusely, sending hands and feet all over the cockpit to make adjustments, and acknowledging the instructor's admonition that I had just lost 10 MPH) I was supposed to say, "Prosser Unicom and Prosser area traffic, this is Cherokee 4258 Juliet on a left downwind for landing on runway 25." I could also ask the Unicom for current wind direction and speed, but there's no time when you are hurtling through the sky at more than 100 miles an hour!

Then there is another wrinkle in flying—something in the air. One time early in my flight training our pattern took us along the edge of southeast Washington's Horse Heaven Hills. Suddenly we hit something that threw me so hard against my seat belt, that my head nearly hit the ceiling. We were bounced around pretty good as the plane dipped and jumped. My eyes must have gotten really big, for I was convinced we would be thrown right out of the sky! Mr. Thompson looked over at me, smiled and said, "Mild turbulence." Mild? I wondered what moderate and severe turbulence would be like! Later I learned how to maintain control in turbulent situations.

About the time I was learning to fly, I was also teaching my son, Sky, to drive a car. I noticed he had the same problems as his flying dad, trying to do everything at once. "Put in the clutch, put it in low gear, ease the clutch out, and at the same time ease down on the accelerator while turning the steering wheel. Now clutch in, foot off accelerator, move gear shift forward halfway then to the right, now forward again. Push down on accelerator, not so hard! Keep looking out the window!"

One thing I learned is that you spare yourself some of the aging process if you don't teach your own kids to drive! The other thing I concluded was that someday, for both of us, all those skills would come together. For me they did on a grand January day in 1976. After a 30-minute lesson, Mr. Thompson got out of the airplane and said, "You're ready. Take it up yourself this time."

Did I really want to do this? Could I really take off, fly and land this plane without somebody there to remind me about everything and help in case of a problem? This was it! I taxied to the end of runway 25, said a hurried prayer, and made my announcement (Pilot Talk, of course): "Prosser area traffic, this is Cherokee 4258 Juliet taking off, runway 25. I'll stay in the pattern, right hand traffic."

I pushed the throttle forward, adjusted the nose wheel on the center line, and waited for the airspeed to build to 60 MPH. Mr. Thompson said with just me in the plane it would take off sooner. But it didn't. The plane seemed to be using more runway than it should. The engine didn't sound exactly right. The airspeed crept to liftoff speed. I pulled back on the yoke and the plane gently lifted off the runway. I was excited and scared at the same time because that engine still sounded different. I quickly checked all instruments. I was not climbing at the normal 750 feet per minute. There were trees at the end of the runway, but I was still climbing so knew I would clear them easily. The airspeed was down a little and the RPMs only 2350. They should have been 2550. What was wrong? "Dear God," I prayed, "let me get this machine back safely to earth!"

Then I spotted it. The carb heat was left on after the last landing. It keeps the carburetor from icing up during the glide for landing. It also reduces the RPM and full engine power needed for takeoff. Now what would I do? If I pushed it in now, Mr. Thompson would know as he heard the engine gain power. I decided that at 400 feet, when I was supposed to reduce power, I would simultaneously reduce carb heat. He would not hear it. That's what I did. He didn't hear it, did he?

As I made my downwind turn at 800 feet, it suddenly hit me. I was way up here by myself! I wanted to just keep going and leave my instructor standing by the runway for a few hours while I took a wondrous scenic trip over hills and valleys. I was free! My dream had come true!

Then I realized I was moving at 100 MPH and needed to prepare for landing this thing. First step, put on that carb heat. I went through the steps, one by one, then lined up on the final approach (I hate that term!). Throttle back, flaps at 20 degrees, trim nose up. Everything looked good. Airspeed 80, perfect. Steady now, full flaps, 100 feet, 75 feet, everything looks good, 50 feet, 25 feet. Now, lift the nose, hold it off, and touchdown! A beautiful full-stall landing, one of my best. Pilots call it *a greaser.*

Dan's first solo, Cherokee 4258 Juliet

Soon after soloing, I bought my own plane. It was a 1953 Piper Tri-Pacer, two-toned green, fabric covered high wing and—most important—major instruments on the right side of the cockpit. I would spend 200 hours in 3501 Alpha.

The next big hurdle in flying was getting my license so I could carry passengers. Would they okay a guy whose body was mostly paralyzed?

I passed my ground school, then the Federal Aviation Administration (FAA) written test with flying colors (pardon the pun). Due to the residuals of polio, I received a waiver from the Federal Flight Surgeon in Oklahoma City. Then I passed the physical exam given to all private pilots. This is required every two years and is called a 3rd Class Medical. Finally, I had to fly with a designated FAA flight examiner to prove my skills were good enough to safely operate a single-engine plane and carry passengers.

On June 15, 1976, just a year and 20 days after my first lesson, I met my examiner from the Spokane General Aviation District Office at the airport in Richland, Washington. After an oral exam, he had me start on a cross-country trip which I had mapped out before take-off. Soon into the flight, he told me a storm was in our route. I was to open my map, take a plotter and pencil, determine a new heading, measure the distance, and draw it on the map. I managed to do it, but had to control the plane, look out the window, and watch the instruments all at the same time, using only one hand to fly, plot, measure and mark.

The examiner wrung me out! He had me close my eyes, then put the plane into "unusual attitudes" (turns, dives, climbs, and combinations). When I opened my eyes he expected me to quickly recognize our situation and recover before becoming inverted or worse!

Then he invented a bad-scene runway situation. He told me to imagine a brick wall across the middle of the runway and 100-foot trees at the front end of it. I was supposed to slip the plane over the trees, land on half the runway, then stop before hitting the brick wall. I brought the plane down beautifully over the trees, leveled off and blasted right through the "fake" brick wall! We both laughed and it relieved the tension a bit. My performance wasn't exactly an "A" on that particular task.

The tests got worse. Near the airport, he pulled back on the throttle to simulate an engine-out landing. I shortened my pattern and set up the best glide speed. I kept the flaps to a minimum until I knew I had the runway "made." I set it up perfectly. Next came full flaps and another "greaser." Just as I started to flare, he yelled, "Go around, go around, don't land!" It's not that easy. Adding full power with the flaps fully deployed causes the nose to point almost straight up. I had to force the

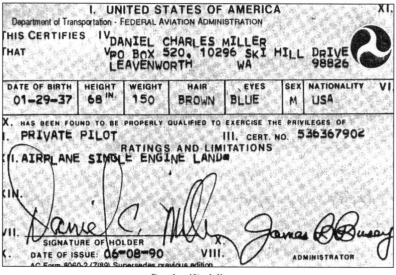

Dan's pilots' license

nose down to gain airspeed, then bleed off the flaps slowly to keep the plane from sinking onto the ground while we were gaining flying speed again. This is where it gets busier than life for a one-armed pilot. Thinking quickly, I threw my chest into the yoke and leaned as far forward as I could to hold the nose down with my chest so the plane would not stall. Then I slowly bled off the flaps, while also adjusting the trim and taking the pressure off my chest. It worked!

Three and a half grueling hours later, I was congratulated, signed off, given my "ticket" and sent home—officially a licensed pilot who could carry passengers. It had been 21 years since polio cancelled my first flying lesson. Judy was waiting for me at the Prosser airport. She climbed in—my first passenger. As the plane lifted off, we both cried as we went on our first flying adventure together. Well, she cried and my eyes sweated.

16

~~~

Pilots Are Just Plane People With a Special Air About Them

Just let me fly

After flying about a year, I offered to take the winner of our church's Sunday school visitor campaign up for a flight. The winner turned out to be the mayor of Prosser, a distinguished gray-haired gentleman who dressed very sharp, maybe because he owned the men's clothing store in town!

Our prize trip took place one Saturday morning. We decided to fly down to Pasco, about 40 miles away from Prosser, in my '53 Tri-Pacer 3501A. On arrival we taxied up to an air service hanger where several pilots were hanging around. I was wearing jeans, a bright shirt and a denim jacket. My passenger looked like he had just stepped out of church. As we got out of the plane I excused myself for a hasty trip to the rest room. When I returned, my friend was talking to these pilots. Since he had been sitting in the usual seat for pilots (remember, I flew right-seat), I thought those pilots might think he was piloting the plane. I was so proud of being able to fly that I wanted to set them straight. I kind of stuck my chest out and gathered courage to announce that I, not my handsome friend, had actually flown this plane. Before I said anything I looked down and noticed that I hadn't buttoned my jacket straight. Worse, my pants were unzipped. Oh, humility. I am glad they *didn't* know I was the pilot!

Dan flew 200 hours in Tri-pacer 3501 alpha

Some of my memorable flights as pilot in command include:

- around and over the top of Mount St. Helens, soon after it blew,
- through the Grand Canyon with Sky, before they restricted private pilots from flying there,
- a 5,000-mile trip around the United States with Sky,

- the Oshkosh Air Show in Wisconsin,
- Nashville, Tennessee,
- circling downtown San Francisco at 1,000 feet,
- down the California coast from San Francisco to Los Angeles at 500 feet,
- over the top of Los Angeles International Airport,
- into Albuquerque, New Mexico, at night,
- circling Mt. Rushmore,
- circling the Hearst Castle in California,
- landing on little old dirt roads in farm country just to see if I could!

I've owned or was a partner in these planes:

- Piper Tri-Pacer (four-place, 135hp),
- two Cessna 150s (two-place, 100 hp),
- Cessna 172 Skyhawk (four-place, 150 hp),
- Piper Cherokee Arrow (four-place, 200 hp, retractable gear, constant-speed prop...FAST!)

Cessna "Superhawk" niner, seven, niner, four, VICTORY!

- Cessna 172 Super Hawk (four-place, 180 hp engine with a constant-speed prop),
- Pterodactyl Ultralight (a hang-glider with a 30 hp snowmobile-type engine)

17

~~~

Any Landing You Walk Away From Is a Good Landing

Close encounters with the ground

Each of these flying machines brought its own challenge, but I learned to be creative in compensating. One of the funnier episodes happened as I was practicing exiting the Tri-Pacer. I startled another pilot passing by as I rolled out of the seat, then flung myself onto the strut, and flipped my body over, landing on the ground with a flop! I told him I had heard one of the requirements for a pilot's license was exiting the plane in five seconds. Since my getting in and out of a plane involved crawling up the low-wing, or grabbing anything I could to flop into a high wing, I decided to invent a new way to get out fast!

I used that procedure one day when my son Sky (who earned his pilot's license at age 17) and I raced a huge Yakima Valley dust storm back to the airport. We spotted the dark wall of dust coming our way when we were ten miles from the airport. We went full throttle with a descending, almost diving, approach. We knew if we didn't beat the storm, we could not land at all. We shot onto runway 07, landed, rolled up to the tie-downs, and both bailed out the doors to tie the plane down. Exactly one minute later 60 MPH winds hit, out of the west, down runway 25—but we were safe, and our plane was securely tied down!

For safety (as well as fun), Sky and I also took spinning lessons. A plane is put into a spin by lifting the nose up until the airplane stops flying and falls – an aerodynamic "stall." As the nose falls down, you kick the rudder and the plane starts spinning towards the ground. There is a way to get out of a spin, and that is mighty nice to know. I never did more than three spins at a time, but Sky and I "practiced" so much that we ruined two gyros. They cost us $200 to replace.

Judy agreed to try a spin with me. As we whipped into that first 360 degrees toward the earth, she calmly said, "That's enough!" That was her first and last spin.

About the closest you can get to flying with the eagles is to sprout your own wings. In 1982 I bought a Pterodactyl Ultralight aircraft, a hang glider with 20-inch bicycle wheels and a snowmobile-type 30-horsepower engine strapped to the back. It had a beautiful rainbow-colored 36 foot wing. I taught myself to fly that thing, since it had room for only one person in it. I would taxi up and down the runway gradually getting enough courage to lift five to ten feet, then ease back the throttle and settle back down. One time I cut the power too much and the ultralight dropped to the runway, breaking the rear axle. I was sitting in the sling unhurt—except for my pride.

I soon was soaring higher and higher, and flying like the birds. I actually had ducks fly formation with me down the Yakima River. A hawk would fly in under my wing occasionally and look me over. I wondered, was it love or anger?

On two separate occasions my engine quit, forcing me into real emergency landings! The first time, I landed in a cow pasture. I had time to choose one without cows. I walked to a farmhouse and

Waving with my foot, Pasco air show, 1983

called for Sky to bring some new spark plugs. We changed plugs, then I took off through tall grass, chopping a swath with the propeller. Roaring into the air, I zoomed over the fence and back to the airport. The next engine-out was over downtown Prosser. Fortunately, I was 600 feet high. The wind direction wouldn't let me head for the airport. I quickly turned with the wind, and that, plus my prayers, helped me glide past trees, houses, and (ugh) the graveyard. I knew I had to glide past my landing spot, then turn into the wind to land. The timing had to be perfect, because I had to make my 180-degree turn before I was 100 feet from the ground. There was a spot just over some power lines at the end of town. Prayer time again! I barely cleared the power lines (I was preparing to dive under them), turned into the wind, and glided to a perfect landing, avoiding an old sagebrush.

That ultralight challenged me again and again. It had no brakes and the only way I could stop quickly was to drag my feet on the ground. I wore out several pairs of shoes over the two years I flew it. In one landing, I was unaware that the wind was blowing sideways. The wind lifted up one wing and the other went down, and off I went on a merry loop on the ground. Dragging my feet was useless. I finally stopped in brush off the runway.

One Saturday I flew about five miles to Whitstran school, where I was principal at the time. While I was working inside, some big winds came off the Horse Heaven Hills, whipping up to 25 MPH. I had to fly that

thing home and I didn't want to! The winds were making me nervous. I had never attempted a flight in winds this strong. I decided I would try it. If it was too turbulent, I would turn around and quickly land. It went up and up like an elevator, but it was pretty smooth. The ultralight could cruise about 35 MPH but barely moved when it

Dan and his Pterodactyl ultralight

headed into that much wind. I ended up "crabbing," at an angle to the wind. It took a long, long time to get back to the airport, and I had to land crosswise on the runway. I landed and stopped in 40 feet. As they say, "mighty short runway, but look how wide it is!"

The big adventure that made me feel like an old-time barnstormer was in July 1983. I packed up some provisions, a tool set, some extra oil (to mix with gas), and headed north from Prosser to Pateros, Washington, over 100 miles away, across mostly uninhabited land. At the half-way point, near the town of Quincy, I started thinking I had better find some fuel. I landed at the Quincy airport only to find the gas pump locked up and no one around. Aviation gas seemed to work best in my engine, so when I saw a spray plane fly by, I took off and followed its flight path. I finally spotted it at a landing strip west of town. I dropped in, bought a couple of gallons of fuel, mixed in the oil, and took off. My flight lasted most of the day as I took sight-seeing side trips, dodged whirlwinds, and inspected canyons. Finally, I reached the mighty Columbia River, flew over it and up to Alta Lake, where I landed on the golf course. The next day, I put on a little air show for the folks at the Pateros Apple Pie Jamboree. I thought of my old pilot friend, Spider Anderson and wished he could see this. Later, we towed the ultralight in the "big" Jamboree parade as people clapped and cheered for that "barnstormer" from somewhere down south.

I liked the ultralight because I could land and take off from almost anywhere. I had two years of adventures in that flying machine. Then two flying buddies were killed in ultralight crashes, including my Pterodactyl's builder. I had flown 71 hours in it. That was enough, so I sold it.

Other planes gave me other types of chills and thrills. One time I was flying with Sky in a Piper Cherokee Arrow, a low-wing plane with retractable wheels. We flew to Pasco and on our return trip lost all electrical power right after takeoff. The battery and alternator weren't doing a thing. That was no problem for the engine since it ran with magnetos, but all the instruments and radios needed the electrical. Besides no radio, we had no lights indicating whether the landing gear was up or down. There is a manual override for the landing gear, so I engaged that.

Sky suggested we fly low along the runway and he could check the plane's shadow to see if they were down. Instead, I thought we'd better return to Pasco and fly a pattern around the airport. I had learned if you did this, the controller will flash lights indicating whether you should go away, continue flying the pattern, or come in for landing. I told Sky the controller would not clear us to land if he did not see the wheels down.

When the controller could not reach us by radio, he used the light gun and brought us in. We got the steady green light which indicated clearance for landing. I brought the plane in, flared it out over the runway and waited for those wheels to touch, hoping I would not end up landing on the belly of the plane. *Finally* they touched and stayed in place. We taxied to an F.B.O. (pilot talk for Fixed Base Operator), phoned the tower, explained our problem, and got clearance to take off again for Prosser with the wheels down and locked all the way.

Another time we flew into Mansfield to visit Grandma and Grandpa Tanneberg for the traditional "Grandpa's Last Birthday" trip. Starting in 1963, when Grandpa turned 80, we had packed the kids in the car for the long drive, advising them, "He's not going to live too many more years." Grandpa celebrated 24 more birthdays, living to age 104! We drove most of those times, but this particular year I decided to fly in. As I turned from base leg onto final approach (there's that term again), the wind swirled around the grain elevators and across the runway, causing an abnormal wind shear. When we were about 75 feet off the ground, with the engine cut all the way back to idle, we hit that unusual air which caused us to sink like crazy. I advanced the throttle, tried to make corrections, and blurted out "hang on" to Judy. She didn't know what to hang on to! I salvaged a pretty nice touchdown and managed to carefully taxi back and tie the plane down. I also learned to keep my mouth shut after that.

I had another sweaty experience on a trip with another one-armed pilot named John Schmerber, who was logging flying hours for his license. We came in to land and winds were howling all around Prosser. I was in the left seat advising him because he, like me, needed to fly left-handed from the right seat. John realized as we were being tossed around coming down "the chute"that he couldn't handle the turbulence, bumps, and cross winds. This situation was a test for any pilot. I took over the controls, set my jaw, and told John, "This one will take both of us, but we can do it." Can't you just see it? Two one-armed bandits, both flying the same plane, in 30-40 MPH gusting crosswinds, sweating profusely, trying to keep their flight path straight down the runway.

John handled the throttle while I manned the controls. Of course, to make matters worse, everyone at or near the airport came out to witness this landing in a windstorm. With me making corrections for the gusts, and John adjusting the throttle and calling out our airspeed every ten seconds, we landed the plane on one wheel, held it against the crosswind, and carefully taxied to the hanger. We did it! Then I realized I was in the wrong seat. We had made a successful, difficult landing, even with me using my "bad" side. That experience gave me confidence, that I could fly an airplane from either seat.

When Sky graduated from high school, he had been a pilot for a year. Sky and I decided we would celebrate by flying across the country. We covered 5,000 miles in a couple weeks. The highlight of the trip was landing at the big air show at Oshkosh, Wisconsin.

Sky and I had taken turns flying, but as we got near Oshkosh, we debated who would land there. It was a big event for a pilot! We decided he would land first and bounce back into the air again, then I would take the controls and land farther down the runway. That way we could both claim we landed at Oshkosh.

When I flew a Cessna 172 from Chicago home to Wenatchee, Washington, I realized that my VORs (navigational radios) weren't working properly. I drifted off course over eastern Montana. That country is so barren that it's hard to figure out where you are. I flew for a while realizing I was not where I was supposed to be. The wind had blown me off course. It was lonely country and getting lonelier by the minute as the plane guzzled fuel. I knew if I flew north, I would eventually find a highway. I did, and followed it until I found a town with its name on the water tank. I looked up the town on my map and was on my way to a nearby airport. Thank goodness for water towers!

Another time Judy and I flew to a breakfast fly-in and air show. As we landed, there were several people close to the runway watching planes come in. Judy was in the usual pilot's seat (since I flew right-seat) and waving happily to people as we settled in five to ten feet off the runway. She said they looked quite shocked, wondering how she, presumably the pilot, could break concentration to do that.

I had flown enough to feel pretty good about my ability to meet emergencies, but the air is always unpredictable. One night Judy and I flew with our friends, Mike and Lois Lyon, to the movies in Kennewick. It was my turn to fly the return trip. As we approached Prosser, some wild winds started coming off the Horse Heaven Hills, producing moderate turbulence. We were a mile from landing, getting knocked around in the air quite a

Pilots are just plane folks

bit, when Mike offered to take over for me. I agreed. It is customary for a pilot to verbalize taking over the controls, so Mike said aloud, "I got it." As he flew down the chute to the runway, he wondered if his offer might have hurt my feelings by implying I couldn't handle it with one arm. Mike would never have said anything negative about my flying skills, so he turned to me and said "You can do this, you take it." I grabbed the yoke, saying "O.K. I have it." From the back seat, came a nervous voice, "Would you make up your minds? One of you needs to land this plane!" I held the speed up a bit to compensate for the gusts and planted the plane firmly on the runway. Another successful landing!

There are times when the radio comes in handy. One time I was flying our Cessna 150 to Fullerton, California, for a national principals' meeting. Following Highway I-5 to land at Vacaville, I noticed my map showed Travis Air Force Base ahead and to my left. I knew its jets had big landing patterns and I didn't want to wander into those. I found the Travis radio frequency on my chart and called up. The controller told me to squawk so-and-so on my transponder. "Negative, I don't have a transponder," I responded. Next he suggested I dial in a certain frequency on my radio. My radio didn't have that frequency. He gave me two more frequencies, and I didn't have those, either! Finally he asked, "How are you navigating?" "I'm looking out the window," I replied. He hesitated and then laughed. "You're all right," he said. "Just keep following that road and you won't be in anybody's way!"

18

~~~

Always Limp with the Same Leg for the Whole Round of Golf

Amazing, but true, golf stories

I wasn't much of a golfer before I had polio. I played maybe twice, just trying it. The first Christmas we were married, Judy gave me a starter golf set. I practiced hitting balls in our yard, swinging right-handed and left-handed with my left hand. I realized I couldn't use two hands except for short chip shots. I got pretty accurate with one arm. Some of my college friends would come over and we would set up a golf course around the house and over the garage.

Then I went to Indian Canyon, a course in Spokane that's rated one of the nicest and toughest in the nation. I took on the back nine, dragging myself and my clubs up and down all sorts of hills. As I struggled up and finished the last hole, my score was 72. That's par for 18 and I had only gone 9 holes! But as I keep saying, *If it's worth doing, it's worth doing poorly at first.* I continued golfing in Spokane, but on flatter courses which better suited my weak legs.

My unorthodox swing brings interesting reactions on the courses. One time I was playing in Bellingham, Washington, with my brother-in-law Vaughn Wolfe. It was a cool day and I wore a long-sleeved sweat shirt, which covered up my paralyzed right arm. Vaughn and I sat at a bench where play had stacked up, waiting our turn. As people came in behind us, we decided to have some fun.

I got up and said, "Can't I hit it with two hands this time? Why do I have to play with one arm?"

"You promised you'd play with one arm," Vaughn replied, enjoying our private joke. "That's only fair."

We got into a big phony argument and finally I yielded to Vaughn. I stepped up with my driver and popped the ball way out there. It was all Vaughn and I could do to suppress laughter as we saw the astonishment of people behind us!

Something similar happened when I played at Leavenworth with a fellow who had suffered a stroke. He swings left-handed with his left hand and I swing right-handed with my left hand. We called ourselves, "One-armed Bandits." One time we both teed off, driving our balls about 150 yards. A fellow standing nearby took off his hat, threw it down, and said, "That does it, I give up!"

When I golf, I sometimes join up with strangers. I usually don't say much, but if they look at me strangely, I say, "I have to hit with one arm." One time after I had hit the ball right down the middle of a narrow fairway, a fellow stepped back and whispered to his partner, thinking I couldn't hear, "I hope I don't get beaten by a one-armed golfer!" I beat both of them. I guess it was my old competitive spirit.

Often when I play with others, they will complain about having a bad day before we even complete the first few holes. "This is my worst game ever," they'll say, or, "I have never played this badly before." Sky says it's the *One Arm Factor.* They do not want to get beaten by a one-armed golfer, so they let it bother them and end up playing less than their best!

Eventually, golf became a big family thing. When we moved to Leavenworth, we started the tradition of a family golf get-together called *The Miller Closed Golf Tournament.*

Relatives are invited each year to a family reunion and two-day golf tourney. We get 35 to 40 people to these reunions, some from states halfway across the nation! We have a huge bronze trophy that so far has been won by the young power-hitters (my son Sky, four times; my son-in-law Brent Harris, and my nephew Damon Sams). We also have trophies for the ladies and grandchildren. I plan to add a new trophy called "Papa's Cup" for the grandkids, to encourage them to practice to play well for this family event.

During this family reunion tournament we build a campfire and sing fun songs and tell stories about the past year. We also have what we call the *Miller A-Fair* to show off our best photos or items made or constructed that year. It's a chance to share our successes and keep our bonds strong as a family.

Although I haven't been able to win the Miller Closed, I have done fairly well for a "one-armed bandit." My balance is poor and my legs are weak, but my short game is very good. I use lighter-weight women's clubs (Ping irons and Callaway Big Bertha woods). I also have a special putter with a shaft high enough to rest my chin on while lining up a putt. A fellow who works on clubs as a hobby designed it and gave it to me. It is long, black and ugly—I call it my "Black and Decker, the Green Wrecker"! Sky says he would rather 3-putt than use that ugly thing! My putting has helped me score well despite my short drives of 100-150 yards. On two occasions in 1996, I had only ten putts on nine holes and have needed only nine putts for nine holes (seven for pars) already in 1997. Last year my handicap dropped to thirteen.

At Leavenworth (Washington) Golf Club, a regulation course, I scored 38 (including six pars) for nine holes and 83 on 18 holes. My other memorable scores were a par 27

Dan shoots an 83, Leavenworth Golf Club

at the Par 3 Pine Acres in Spokane, and a one-over-par 29 on the front and one over par 31 on the back at Village Greens Golf Course in Port Orchard, Washington.

I have fun golfing. Once I played in an administrators' golf tournament called the "Open Minded Golf Tournament." I won the biggest trophy called "Best One-Armed Golfer." (I ordered the trophies that year—sometimes you have to look out for yourself!)

In the summer, when I golf in shorts and a tank top, I'm a sight to behold. Polio doesn't leave you with a body-builder physique. I would make a good "before" picture for those muscle-builder advertisements, but I don't care. I am there to relax, enjoy and surprise myself. Like the day in April, 1996, when I took my friend Mike Lyon golfing at the Village Greens Golf Club. On the 135-yard Hole #3, I chose a 7 wood. We watched my drive roll down the hill, bounce onto the green, and then disappear into

The one arm bandit!
Showing how he hit his hole in one
photo by Eric Blais

the cup. It was a hole-in-one! Talk about dreams coming true. I will do it again, too—just you wait. I'm so positive about another one, I've chosen not to play alone, so I will always have a witness!

19

I'm Their Leader—Which Way Did They Go?

School and the principal of the place

In 1979, I switched from teaching PE to elementary administration, becoming a principal at Prosser in southeast Washington state. After six years as an administrator at Prosser, I moved to Osborn Elementary School in Leavenworth, Washington. In 1988, I was given one of eight state Excellence in Education Principal awards. In 1987 and 1989, I received one of seven state Distinguished Principal awards. I'm not sure what they had in mind when they called me "distinguished" because our school had a reputation for being zany. I had a sign on my office door that said, "Take your profession seriously, but don't take yourself seriously."

I did take my job too seriously at first. As a new principal in Prosser, I focused on the problems. I let the paperwork and pressures pull me down and make me a bit grumpy. In fact, within several months I ended up in the hospital all stressed out. I tell people that I still have the note my staff sent me: *Dear Dan, We wish you a speedy recovery. The vote was 21-19!*

That's when I decided to choose to enjoy life at school in spite of the problems. I had forgotten to laugh and have fun. I wanted a positive, fun atmosphere. To combat the negative and create the positive, I had to start with me. After all, I was the leader! At Leavenworth we started a "Laugh Committee" and flooded the school with one-liner jokes:

If your cow doesn't give milk, sell him.

Marry me, and I'll never bother you again.

I've used up all my sick leave, so tomorrow I'm calling in dead.

Dust is a protective covering for furniture.

I'd like to live in the fast lane, but I'm married to a speed bump! (Judy's favorite!)

If your parents didn't have any children, chances are you won't have any either.

You are what you eat, so I eat only rich foods.

If the good Lord had wanted us to bend over, He would have put chocolate on the floor.

I posted them in the restrooms, over the copy machine, and many other places you wouldn't expect.

I worked extra hard at making the school bulletin fun, adding quips and outrageous stories about my golf score or my wife's red sports car. I would retell classic jokes and substitute staff names:

Mr. Miller: This old school clock in my office will run seven days without winding.

Mrs. Rayfield [my secretary]: That's great! How long will it run if you wind it?

My bulletins contained word puzzles, elephant jokes and brain teasers. Another favorite entry:

A mother was having a hard time getting her son to go to school in the morning.

"Nobody likes me in school," he complained. "The teachers don't like me, the kids don't like me, the superintendent wants to transfer me, the bus drivers hate me, the school board wants me to drop out, and the custodians have it in for me. I don't want to go to school."

"But you have to go to school," countered his mother. "You are healthy, you have lots to learn, you have something to offer others, you are a leader. And besides, you are the principal!"

My staff started crazy traditions. On the last Thursday before the last Friday, before the last day of school, we had "The Last Supper." There was an OTLB (Out To Lunch Bunch) staff fun group at my school. They would plan fun get-togethers during the year.

On school picture day, I really hammed it up by wearing something unusual. One year I wore plastic rabbit teeth for my official picture. I had the pictures enlarged and displayed in the hallway as "Portraits of the Principal."

I patrolled the playground on a small Honda Trail 70 motor bike. I called it "Harley Honda." The kids called it "Hardly a Honda"! One year I rode it into the opening assembly. I roared down the hall, into the gym, and around the kids, then took off my helmet and said. "I'm your principal, Mr. Miller. We are going to have a great year." The kids' eyes got big and so did the teachers'!

In the winter we had rules about not throwing snowballs, but I knew how tough it was for kids to refrain. So once in a while I would declare a Snowball Recess and venture out with myself as a permissible target. Some of the kids had pretty strong arms. They loved hitting me with snowballs!

I would also wear silly stuff to school. I had a collection of more than 200 buttons to pin on my shirt or coat.

They had wonderful thoughts about life, such as:
My brain is writing checks my body can't cash.
If your phone doesn't ring, you'll know it's me.
Does the noise in my head bother you?
I'm too young to be this old.
New clinical studies show there are no answers.

*Patrolling the playground
with "Harley"*

A smile is a crooked line that straightens out a lot of things!

Money is the root of all evil. Send $9.95 for more information.

I had silly neckties, such as one that looked like a skeleton hand (it went with a "bonehead" hat). I called it my "hand-me-down tie." I figured out how to wear almost anything as a tie. In October I would wear a rubber skeleton. In December I wore a stuffed Rudolph which would play a favorite Christmas song when I pulled its feet down.

I also had a large, crazy hat collection. Each was unique and got the kids smiling and their eyes sparkling. My favorite was built by one of our district custodians. Steve Vaughn took a logger's hard hat, hooked on wings made out of helicopter blades, mounted blinking lights and engines with props that whirled at the flick of a switch. I would put on this hat, stride into a classroom, and disrupt all education. I had another hat with clapping hands operated by a string so I could give the kids "a hand" for any success.

Other hats featured various animals, including my deer-head "hunting hat." My motto was—the sillier, the better. I wore these hats to school "Celebrations," which parents and grandparents attended. One parent who ran a shop in downtown Leavenworth decided to open a hat shop and came to inspect my collection for ideas. The store became a big success.

Principal Dan and his "hand-me-down tie"

I also had special noses and ears I would put on just before someone came into my office. They never knew what to expect.

And then there were slippers. I wore slippers inside during the winter when I had to wear huge snow boots to school. Off came the boots, on would go my furry "bear feet" slippers. My favorite outfit was my "Just Ducky" hat and matching duck-feet slippers, which I wore to every kindergarten parent orientation.

Sometimes when I wore these outfits, sales people came into the building and would walk right past me, never suspecting that I was the principal. At Halloween we always went crazy with costumes. At Prosser I added a long-haired wig to go with my beard, held it on with a

117

red bandana and added the leather and chains to look like Willie Nelson. My secretary always dressed up special as well. The office was a fun place to visit. Another year I moussed and spiked my hair into a mohawk and wore (ouch!) bull clips for earrings. Still another time I painted my face white, sprayed my hair red, and added holey, scruffy denim to become "Boy Dan," my version of the punk rock star Boy George. That same day some parents came to the superintendent to complain about a bus driver. He had to call "Boy Dan" in to talk to them. They were so mad they didn't even smile or laugh at my outlandish outfit. And I had on a button that said, "*Is that your face, or did your neck throw up?*" I'm sure they wondered what kind of principal the district had hired.

I had a great staff with a great attitude, but not everyone was perky on Mondays. They probably saw the negative sign that says, "On Monday I rise and whine." I told my staff from now on Monday would be the greatest day of the week. After all, it is one-seventh of our lives and one-fifth of our work week. The staff reacted by wearing black the next Monday. I persisted. I put up signs that said, "I Live for Monday" and "TGIM"(Thank God it's Monday). I added reminders to Friday school bulletins: "Only two and one half days until Monday." Eventually, Monday became a popular day in our school (well, maybe for a couple of us). I have found hating Monday is a national problem, so I continue my battle to elevate its status. I have even changed my phone number to include the letters "TGIM"!

One of education's worst images is that of the kid called or sent to the principal's office. I told my staff—everybody from cooks to teachers—to start noticing kids who were doing things right and send them to me in the principal's office.

So students started trooping in carrying notes saying an adult had noticed a change in their behavior or better work on school assignments. Maybe they had finished a hard book, done a kind deed, or simply been a good kid who did what was expected. I had a big home-made book I called the *Good Kids Book* on display in the office. When the kids were sent in, they signed this book with big colored markers. Then I gave them a penny to get some jelly beans I kept in an old gum machine. Finally, I had them wait while I called a parent or grandparent at home or work to brag on their "good" achievement.

Parents are usually afraid of any call from the school, especially from the principal. Their past experience was that such calls meant a child was hurt, sick, or in trouble. But word of the "good kid" calls spread throughout the community. A Seattle television station even came over and did a special on it.

I always got through to parents, even when a secretary had to interrupt a parent in a meeting. One time I couldn't get a student's parents at home or work. The little guy suggested I call his grandma.

"Where does she live?" I asked.

"Mexico," he said. Fortunately, he couldn't remember the phone number. The last year I was at Leavenworth, there were more than 3,300 "good kids" visits to my office.

Behavioral scientists say your productivity goes up when you are around happy people. I agree with that. Our offbeat, happy school lifestyle seemed to ease tensions in the staff and create a comfortable learning environment for children. And the children's academic test scores improved every year.

We also worked on improving communication. So many times we herd kids from here to there, but they also need time just to talk to adults. One survey at a Washington high school revealed that the students' greatest need was a meaningful conversation with an adult.

The Good Kids Book

Deciding this was just as true for elementary students, I urged my staff to use their playground time to chat with students about their horses or bikes or whatever else. My silly buttons, hats, ties, and slippers gave children an excuse to talk to me. Focusing on an "unstuffy" environment helped build trust. When children really had something to talk about, they felt they could approach us.

Another educator gave me the idea for the WIF Button Award. At each weekly assembly he would call up four to five children. While pinning on a big "WIF" button, he would whisper in the child's ear "What It's For" (hence the initials)—usually a character quality.

Curious classmates and teachers had to later ask the student why he won the button.

Another project that helped boost kids' self-esteem was the toy checkout program. We had a wonderful group in Leavenworth which spent hundreds of dollars each year for winter coats and Christmas presents for the school's needy. One year I asked them for additional money to buy some expensive toys. At that time, Cabbage Patch® dolls and Transformers® were the toys every kid wanted. Some of the kids in our school had them, but some came from homes where the money didn't stretch far enough to buy them. So I filled my office with these new, expensive toys and set up a program in which children with good behavior, as measured by the five school goals, could take a dreamed-about toy home for a few days. (After I was finished playing with them!)

20

Will Speak For Food

Following dreams—encouraging others to do the same

While I was still a principal, I would try to encourage students by sharing stories about my struggles and dreams. I was also asked to share with other educators some of the positive things going on at our school. I enjoyed it and the audiences listened and laughed. In 1989, I had some physical problems my doctor thought might be related to post-polio syndrome. He advised me to ease up. So at the age of 53, I retired after 28 years in public education, hoping to supplement our income with some public speaking. (I tell people I didn't retire, I surrendered!)

Did somebody say "retire"?

In the first six years, I ended up speaking to more than 250,000 people in 25 different states. Several thousand more around the world heard my story when it was aired by Focus on the Family, the radio broadcast sponsored by psychologist and author Dr. James Dobson. We have never advertised ourselves as speakers. We have no bureau we work through, but our calendar has filled up and we are on the road or in the air more than we are home, giving as many as a hundred presentations a year.

As I travel throughout the country, I give people the same message I gave my students and that Dr. Hagelin gave me long ago as a scared but determined college freshman: "Let's see what you can do." I encounter a lot of people who are handicapped in ways other than physical. Many are crippled by poor self-esteem. I tell them that if they like and accept themselves, others will like them too. A healthy self-esteem grows from choices we make. Over and over I say:

Remember, it's not what you look like, it's who you are.

Never put yourself down.

You are special, unique, and important!

I also tell people that nobody can predict what you can do. No one has the right to destroy your dreams. All of us will have tough times in life. We will experience sorrow, heartache, pain, and suffering. But there will also be JOY! We can choose to be miserable or opt for JOY! I know that because it has worked for me.

After I spoke at a business meeting, someone came up and said, "Whenever I hear speakers on success, they emphasize money and how to get more. You emphasize how to live. That's what success really is."

I remember a third grade girl who came to my school in Leavenworth. She lived with her grandmother and transferred from a small private school. She had physical and developmental problems and was very scared coming to a school with nearly 400 kids.

After she had grown and graduated from high school, her grandmother told me, "You were her dreammaker. You encouraged her and told her she could do it. We walked out of your office encouraged, uplifted, and accepted." In an essay her granddaughter wrote as a high school senior, she remembered, "Mr. Miller encouraged me and taught me to smile and believe in myself."

Proverbs 11:25 says "He who refreshes others will himself be refreshed." Getting feedback like that keeps me going and going, eager to infuse peoples' lives with hope and humor and encouragement.

"I Lobster but Never Flounder."

125

21

Misery Is Optional–
Joy Is a Choice

Focus on what you can do

In the fall of 1996, Judy and I got a rather unexpected memo from a school district in Texas. Someone had seen a video of my "Dreammaker" presentation and passed it on to a school counselor, who, after seeing it, showed my story to more than 250 children in grades four through six. Every October this school has a "Great Americans" week during which they feature the biographies of famous people in the nation's history and focus on positive character traits. Part of the reason for this is to help children make wise choices when confronted with negative influences such as drugs, alcohol, and tobacco.

A highlight of the 1996 week was a play in which these students honored the great Americans Abraham Lincoln, Johnny Appleseed, Helen Keller, Nolan

Ryan...and me! It was humbling and a real honor to be chosen.

I guess I represent thousands who have dealt with handicaps. I know the frustrations of being a one-armed, weak-legged person. Sometimes even putting on a belt can be aggravating. Just try reaching around your waist with one arm and putting that belt through the loops! A lot of fix-it or mechanical jobs are too much for me. I know how, but they are two-handed tasks. I can't hold a nail in one hand and pound with a hammer in the other. It's no fun taking an hour on a job that should take ten minutes, because you have to hold something with your teeth or figure out another way to do it with one hand.

Although there are many things I cannot do, or are very difficult to do, I am thankful for what I have. *My focus has not been on what I can't do but on what I can do.* So far in my life I have:

♥ married Judy and loved and laughed with her since 1959,

♥ became a father to Sky, Danica, and Karmen—great kids who overcame their own health challenges,

♥ taught fifth and sixth grades,

♥ taught elementary physical education for kindergarten through sixth grade,

♥ served as a middle school athletic director, vice principal, and student council advisor,

♥ led schools as an elementary principal for eleven years,

♥ coached middle school/junior high football, baseball, softball, track, and basketball,

♥ earned a real estate license and sold real estate for several years,

♥ bought, managed, and sold both a motel and an apartment building,

♥ worked as a park ranger and tour guide at Grand Coulee Dam,

♥ played and sang in a band which made its own recording,

♥ taught guitar lessons (I had 21 students a week),

♥ taught bass guitar lessons,

♥ flown and owned or co-owned seven planes, including an ultralight,

♥ operated several types of power boats,

♥ ridden motorcycles, including the BIG ONES,

♥ driven trucks, bulldozers, and tractors,

♥ fished and hunted—and missed a deer!

♥ water-skied a whole 100 yards!

♥ snow-skied, sort of! I took some wild spills but at least I tried it!

♥ bowled,

♥ danced (I do slow dances best),

♥ spoken more than 800 times to groups ranging from five to 9,000 people,

♥ spoken in 27 states or Canadian provinces,

♥ written a book,

♥ <u>and</u> there is more to come!

22

~~~

Living the Abun**DAN**t Life

What God has done

The heart of my story is not what Dan Miller has done. It is what God has done. God is my great Dreammaker. All I have or have achieved has come through Him.

I had the privilege of growing up in a home where my parents took my sisters and me to church. When I was ten years old, an evangelist visited our church and explained that being born into a Christian family didn't make you a Christian. He asked those who wanted to become Christians by their own decision to come to the altar and pray. I was one who did.

When polio put me on my back, I knew God was my only hope. I asked Him to help me recover and achieve my dreams. Later on at college, I got so busy with school, sports, work, and proving myself, that God was nudged aside.

Eventually, I realized that all these activities and achievements did not provide a deep, inner satisfaction.

After Judy and I married, we decided to begin attending church. Judy had no church background. We chose to visit her obstetrician's church. The music was nice, the sermons appealed to my intellectual side, but something very important was missing. They seldom mentioned Jesus Christ.

When we moved to Bellingham, Washington, we visited the same type of church. Again, something seemed to be missing—no mention of Jesus.

I was focusing on scaling the ladder of educational success. My next step was my doctorate. Being around successful people was important to me, so we decided to visit a large nearby church, which many important people attended. Joining would have been easy. The minister met with several of us interested in church membership. After summarizing the church history and the joining procedure, he asked each of us, "Do you want to join the church?"

All nodded yes. But not me.

I had seen and heard enough to realize there was an emptiness in this particular church. The people were nice, but their lives did not seem to reflect whether they knew God or not.

I had reached a point in my life where I was searching for inner peace and joy—something beyond myself or what I could achieve. This minister did not seem to really know God. He would hide little notes in the pulpit and collection plate, and then read his prayers to God. I watched him like a hawk when my eyes were supposed to be closed.

My refusal to join startled him.

"Why not?" he asked.

"Because I don't think joining this church will change anything inside me," I said firmly.

My quest to really know God led me to the public library where I checked out several books on religion. I needed answers to the big questions:

Who am I?

Where am I going?

If there is a God, how would He communicate with me?

Then we bought a home in a neighborhood where several families kept inviting us to their church, Immanuel Bible. By then, I wanted our three children in Sunday school. I knew what I had learned as a boy was important in family training. We visited and were impressed by how these people genuinely cared for us. I liked the pastor, Jerry Wilson. He had a great sense of humor and would joke about his crooked nose. He had that deep-down realness I wanted. He kept talking about Jesus Christ. He quoted all the time from the Bible. I felt I was getting closer to my answers about life.

We kept attending this church, and heard how God loves us and communicated with us by sending His Son Jesus Christ. That's what I learned as a boy when I memorized John 3:16. Now it was making sense for me, personally.

One Sunday Pastor Jerry quoted, *"Behold, I stand at the door and knock. If any man hears my voice and opens the door, I will come in to him and sup with him and he with me"* (Revelation 3:20 KJV).

I realized Christ was knocking quietly at the door to my heart. Judy heard the same knock. She was in tears, realizing she had missed these truths all her life. Before this she thought that being an American made you a Christian.

That night, Judy and I both prayed and asked Jesus to take over our lives. I didn't need books on religion after that. The Bible became a living, personal book. I could sense God talking to me as I read it and began to apply His principles to my life. One big change came as I considered Ephesians 2:8-9. Those verses told me God's offer of salvation was His gift, not dependent on anything I tried to do to earn his favor. That freed me from thinking I needed to go for a doctorate, earn lots of money, or be with important people to be in God's favor.

In the years to follow, Judy and I found the Bible relevant to our lives. We opened our home to Good News Clubs for children and home Bible studies. We taught Sunday school and served as camp counselors.

God has richly blessed our family. Our children chose wonderful spouses and have blessed us with eight awesome grandchildren.

There is one verse in the Bible that seems to summarize my life as Dan Miller, polio survivor; *"Now unto Him Who, by the power that is at work within us, is able to do superabundantly, far over and above all that we[dare] ask or think—infinitely beyond our highest prayers, desires, thoughts, hopes or dreams—"* (Ephesians 3:20 Amplified).

That verse has my name in it—see the "Dan" in "superabunDANtly"? God really has done "super abundantly" in my life. He has helped me achieve goals which some people considered impossible.

There is another verse I see as describing my life and that's one that talks about my handicap. The apostle Paul had a handicap. He prayed for that handicap to be taken away. But God left it with him. Despite all the prayers on my behalf, my body never returned to normal. I will have limitations all the rest of my earthly life. (I sometimes joke with folks, "Please don't pray for me to be healed. It will ruin my speaking career!") But I put them in Paul's perspective, expressed in 2 Corinthians. I like how Eugene Peterson puts it into contemporary English:

Papa Dan and his grandkids

"…*I was given the gift of a handicap to keep me in constant touch with my limitations….At first I didn't think of it as a gift, and begged God to remove it. Three times I did that, and then he told me, 'My grace is enough; it's all you need. My strength comes into its own in your weakness.' Once I heard that, I was glad to let it happen. I quit focusing on the handicap and began appreciating the gift*" (2 Corinthians 12: 7-9 The Message).

I didn't always think of my handicap as a "gift," but now I see how it has changed my life for the better. My life has been filled with wonderful caring people and challenging adventures that I would have missed as a "normal" person. I have lived an exciting, abundant life here on earth. And because my relationship with God will last forever, I have an eternity of wonderful Mondays to look forward to!

The Author

Dan Miller is a retired educator. He has a master's degree in education from Eastern Washington University. He was a teacher, P.E. specialist and school principal. Dan received two Washington Distinguished Principal awards and the Excellence in Education Award from the Governor of Washington State.

Dan began full-time speaking in 1990, and has shared his inspirational story with more than 250,000 people in person and thousands more on Dr. James Dobson's *Focus on the Family* radio program. He also was featured on Dr. Robert Schuller's *Hour of Power* television program. His story is available on videotape.

Dan's message of hope, humor, and encouragement has entertained people from all walks of life: students, church groups, schools, businesses, hospitals and a variety of associations.

Dan and Judy, married since 1959, also present seminars on building positive attitudes and being "Dreammakers." These presentations are available on audiotape.

Dan and Judy have three terrific children and eight beautiful, awesome, talented, gifted, fantastic grandchildren. The Millers live near Seattle, Washington.

Contact Dan & Judy at:
2485 Alaska Ave. E.
Port Orchard, WA 98366
(360) 871-TGIM, fax (360) 871-2507
e-mail danmiller@telebyte.com
Web page available July 1997
Comments welcome

About Jeanne Zornes

Jeanne Zornes lives in the apple-heart of Washington state—a town called Wenatchee. She and her teacher-husband Richard have two teenage children, Zachary and Inga. Jeanne is author of *When I Prayed for Patience...God Let Me Have It!* (Harold Shaw, 1995) and *The Power of Encouragement* (Moody Press, 1982). She's also contributed to ten other books and published more than 500 magazine articles, short stories, and devotionals. She's spoken at retreats and meetings in the Pacific Northwest about living for Christ in a discouraged and discouraging world. For more information on her conference topics, you can contact her at 1025 Meeks St., Wenatchee, WA 98801.

***Put some fun
into your next meeting!***

Presentations:
by Dan & Judy Miller

1. Living Laughing,
& Loving Life!

2. Dreammaker
-be one!

3. The Attitude
Advantage

**Call:
(360) 871-TGIM!**

If you like this book, you will love this other fun stuff. Order now.

Name:

Address:

City:

State/Province: Zip/Postal

Telephone:

item	price x	quantity	amount
Living, Laughing & Loving Life—Book	$ 9.95		
Living, Laughing & Loving Life—Video	$ 29.95		
Living, Laughing & Loving Life—Audio	$ 9.95		
One Liners: Silly Sayings	$ 4.95		
Dreammaker—Be One Judy's Booklet	$ 3.95		
Subtotal			
Shipping			$ 3.00
Priorities Poster (11X14) shipping included	$ 8.00		
Washington Residents Sales Tax 8.2%		8.2%	
Total Payment			$

Make checks or money orders payable to: Judy Miller, Box 55, Manchester, WA 98353, or call (360) 871-TGIM

If you like this book, you will love this other fun stuff. Order now.

Name:	
Address:	
City:	
State/Province:	Zip/Postal
Telephone:	

item	price x	quantity	amount
Living, Laughing & Loving Life—Book	*$ 9.95*		
Living, Laughing & Loving Life—Video	*$ 29.95*		
Living, Laughing & Loving Life—Audio	*$ 9.95*		
One Liners: Silly Sayings	*$ 4.95*		
Dreammaker—Be One Judy's Booklet	*$ 3.95*		
Subtotal			
Shipping			*$ 3.00*
Priorities Poster (11X14) shipping included	*$ 8.00*		
Washington Residents Sales Tax 8.2%		*8.2%*	
Total Payment			*$*

Make checks or money orders payable to: Judy Miller,
Box 55, Manchester, WA 98353, or call (360) 871-TGIM